Discover the Holy Spirit

Overcome the Unholy World

Sandra F. McClure

A message for the Unbeliever, the Unsure, and the Uninformed

Discover the Holy Spirit - Overcome the Unholy World

Trilogy Christian Publishers

A Wholly Owned Subsidiary of Trinity Broadcasting Network

2442 Michelle Drive, Tustin, CA 92780

Copyright © 2024 Sandra F. McClure

Scripture quotations marked (NASB) are taken from the New American Standard Bible® (NASB), Copyright © 1960, 1962, 1963, 1968, 1971, 1972, 1973, 1975, 1977, 1995 by The Lockman Foundation. Used by permission. www.Lockman.org.

Scripture quotations marked (NIV) are taken from the Holy Bible, New International Version®, NIV®. Copyright © 1973, 1978, 1984, 2011 by Biblica, Inc.™ Used by permission of Zondervan. All rights reserved worldwide. www.zondervan.com. The "NIV" and "New International Version" are trademarks registered in the United States Patent and Trademark Office by Biblica, Inc.™

Scripture quotations marked (ESV) are taken from the ESV® Bible (The Holy Bible, English Standard Version®), copyright © 2001 by Crossway Bibles, a publishing ministry of Good News Publishers. Used by permission. All rights reserved.

For information, address Trilogy Christian Publishing Rights Department, 2442 Michelle Drive, Tustin, CA 92780.

Trilogy Christian Publishing/ TBN and colophon are trademarks of Trinity Broadcasting Network.

For information about special discounts for bulk purchases, please contact Trilogy Christian Publishing.

Trilogy Disclaimer: The views and content expressed in this book are those of the author and may not necessarily reflect the views and doctrine of Trilogy Christian Publishing or the Trinity Broadcasting Network.

10 9 8 7 6 5 4 3 2 1

Library of Congress Cataloging-in-Publication Data is available.

ISBN: 979-8-89041-764-0

ISBN: 979-8-89041-765-7

Dedication

This book is dedicated to adult seekers of truth.
May God bless your quest.

Acknowledgments

All living creatures are given a finite number of minutes, hours, and days on the earth. May I never take it for granted when someone gives away a portion of his or her lifetime to encourage me, to pray for me, or to help me endure life's hardships.

To Bill McClure – Your eternal optimism and encouragement in this writing enabled me to keep going, free from stress or guilt. Thank you for your sweet, supportive love and companionship always! I'm so thankful God brought us together!

To Linda Silva and Margie Mangham, my precious sisters: We know each other so well, and love each other so deeply. We shared much time in the trenches, but through the power of the Holy Spirit, we crawled out victorious with joy, love, and laughter that vastly overshadow the trench experiences. No one on earth knows me better but loves me anyway! You inspire me, encourage me, and lift me up when I need a boost (and that's not easy!). Thank you for listening with loving, honest ears! You're both skilled communicators, and I trust your judgment in every writing project I pursue.

To Rebecca Goldsmith – Your encouragement and prayer support in this project made it possible! I cherish your friendship and feel so blessed to know I always have a prayer warrior willing to lift my name to our Heavenly Father.

To the precious friends who have prayed for me or encouraged me over the years – you have kept the commandment to *carry one another's burdens*. I am blessed and so thankful for your friendship.

And to my pastor of forty years, Michael D. Woods, I am forever grateful for your wise and thoughtful counsel in this project. Your selfless, God-centered leadership has blessed three generations of my family and countless others. The residual impact of your anointed shepherding will continue to bless generations to come.

I love you all and thank God for placing each one of you in my life!

Introduction

The person without the Spirit does not accept the things that come from the Spirit of God, but considers them foolishness, and cannot understand them because they are discerned only through the Spirit.

1 Corinthians 2:14 (NIV)

This book is written for those described in the above message found in the Word of God. Those of us in whom the Holy Spirit inhabit know these words to be true. We seem to be the only social group deemed fair game to public mockery and ridicule. Relegated to our Sunday school classes and private Bible studies, we're being pushed underground. Let's not forget the Covid pandemic when churches were forced to close, but liquor stores were open. I ask those who believe the message of Christians to be *foolishness,* to read these pages with the open mind that Christians are so often accused of lacking. But there is one caveat: It will require you to at least consider that God's Word is the inerrant, all-sufficient guide necessary to understanding this world and your place in it. Consider it an experiment if you like. I'm not worried about your response because it's not my job to convince you; it's the Holy Spirit's. I am simply attempting to follow the sage advice of Dr. Charles Stanley: *Obey God and leave the consequences to Him.* Whether a believer in God's sovereignty or not, I ask you to call on God to reveal truth to you. It only takes a mustard seed of faith (Matthew 17:20), so open your heart and mind a mustard seed's worth to give truth a chance. After all, knowing the truth sets us free (John 8:32). If you can't muster a mustard seed, I ask you to at least pass this book on to someone who might.

If you're willing to give it a shot, I suggest you shut out all preconceived ideas about God, Christians, the Bible, church, and political affiliations. Just read with an open mind. I'll be praying for you, and if you become a believer in the process, let's make a plan to celebrate for all eternity!

Our world is spiritually dying, and we all need to understand why – and learn what we can do about it.

The 2021 number of deaths by suicide in the United States is reported to be 48,183. That's one suicide every eleven minutes.

- » 12.3 million adults seriously thought about suicide.
- » 3.5 million adults made a plan to commit suicide.
- » 1.7 million adults attempted suicide. [1]

What should that tell us about our culture? It tells me we need help. Suicide is the ultimate act of desperation and hopelessness. Let me get this out of the way; I am not an authority on the subject. However, my lack of formal education on a subject has never prevented me from having an opinion on said subject. With that said, it is my opinion that the vast majority of suicidal deaths, homicidal deaths, and for that matter, every crime and dysfunction in our society, are the result of a spiritual problem. Why do I believe this? Because we are spiritual creatures, made with the inherent need for guidance from the Spirit of God.

Just think of all the time, money, heartache, broken families, and broken lives that might be saved if our society would just give this idea serious consideration. What have we got to lose?

It's a Spiritual Problem!
The Solution is Free!

Table of Contents

Chapter 1: We Are Spirit   11
Chapter 2: The Evil Spirit   25
Chapter 3: Supreme Court Spirit   43
Chapter 4: Aftermath of Engel v. Vitale   53

A Poem Inspired by the Spirit:
The Information Age   69

Chapter 5: Getting to Know the Holy Spirit   71
Chapter 6: The Omnipresence of the Holy Spirit   89
Chapter 7: Sinning Against the Holy Spirit   97

Epilogue/Final Thoughts   107
Notes/Citations   109

Chapter 1

We are Spirit

We are not human beings having a spiritual experience; we are spiritual beings having a human experience.[2]

Before we proceed, I ask you to take a moment to let this simple, but profound truth wash over you and seep into the depths of your being.

This quote is attributed to the French Jesuit priest, scientist, and philosopher Pierre Teihard de Chardin (1881-1955). Although he died a year before my birth, his words still impact me today as I ponder so many mysteries in this world. I can't even tell you where or when I first heard this quote, but I can only determine that the God of the universe, and Lord of my life wanted me to hear it and share it, so here I am, in my 66th year, sharing it with anyone else willing to hear it.

With the Covid pandemic in our rear-view mirror, we can now recall with clearer minds, the indoctrination of our culture into the religion of science. I wish I had a nickel for every time we were told to *Follow the science*, or *Trust the science*, yet the results of following the science proved to be immeasurably detrimental to our culture in this generation, and who knows how many generations to follow.

It's Not a Scientific Answer, But a Spiritual One

Let's see what one of the most brilliant scientific minds of all time, Albert Einstein, has to say about spirit:

Everyone who is seriously engaged in the pursuit of science becomes convinced that the laws of nature manifest the existence of a spirit vastly superior to that of men, and one in the face of which we with our modest powers must feel humble. [3]

We are made in the image of our creator, God (Genesis 1:27). God is spirit, and we are spiritual creatures. Once we grasp that truth, only then can we glean a smidgen of understanding about what is happening in the world around us. Perhaps it's hard to grasp the spiritual world because we function in the physical realm (by sight) and the only way to fully understand spiritual matters, to the extent our earthly comprehension will allow, is to access the Holy Spirit, one of the three persons of the Trinity. Jesus explains it in His beautiful figurative language, in response to a Pharisee named Nicodemus. A Pharisee was a member of the Jewish ruling council called the Sanhedrin. Nicodemus came to Jesus under the cover of night, probably fearful that he would be ridiculed for humbling himself to approach this enigmatic man seen performing many miracles to include healing the sick, walking on water, calming the storm, feeding thousands with one little boy's lunch, casting out demons, and even raising the dead. How could this religious leader not examine this man more closely? Please consider this portion of the conversation between Jesus and Nicodemus in John, chapter 3:2-6, 8:

*He came to Jesus at night and said, Rabbi, we know you are a teacher who has come from God. For no one could perform the miraculous signs you are doing if God were not with him. In reply, Jesus declared, I tell you the truth, no one can see the Kingdom of God unless he is born again. How can a man be born when he is old? Nicodemus asked. Surely he cannot enter a second time into his mother's womb to be born! Jesus answered, I tell you the truth, no one can enter the kingdom of God unless he is born of water **and** the Spirit. Flesh gives birth to flesh, but the Spirit gives birth to spirit...The wind blows wherever it pleases. You hear its sound but you cannot tell where it comes from or where it is going. So it is with everyone born of the Spirit.*

Jesus continues His conversation with this powerful religious leader, further explaining in more literal terms, the most valuable information ever spoken to mankind:

For God so loved the world that He gave his one and only Son, that whosoever believes in Him shall not perish, but have eternal life. For God did not send His Son into the world to condemn the world, but to save the world through him. Whoever believes in Him is not condemned, but whoever does not believe stands condemned already, because he has not believed in the name of God's one and only Son.

John 3:16-18

In a nutshell, we receive the Holy Spirit by receiving Jesus. They are one with the Father. And through no effort of our own, other than accepting the gift, we are saved from the punishment of death. Nicodemus didn't need help believing in Jesus intellectually. He clearly stated he believed Jesus was from God because he witnessed the miraculous signs that could only come from God. But Jesus addressed his need. Nicodemus needed to believe not with his head, but with his heart – his spirit. Today is no different. Spiritual needs are more prevalent than ever, but we tend to search for spiritual answers with scientific questions. That is futile thinking. But I ask you to stop here before reading any further. Ask God, whether a believer or not, to give you understanding of this next scripture.

In God's message to us, the First book of Corinthians, Chapter 2, Verse 14 explains: *The person without the Spirit does not accept the things that come from the Spirit of God, but considers them foolishness, and cannot understand them because they are discerned only through the Spirit.*

Conversely, the person *with* the indwelling of the Holy Spirit is capable of discerning spiritual matters, and even capable of having a personal relationship with his or her creator, through the acceptance of Jesus Christ. Spirit communes with spirit. And the fruits of that indwelling are so vast and so beautiful; my human words can't do them justice! I'm reminded of the *I love you to the moon ...* game my pre-school daughter and I would play: *I love you to the moon; I love you to the moon and back; I love you to the moon and back and back again.* You get the idea. She finally replied, *I love you so much I can't describe it!* That's how I'm feeling now as I make a feeble attempt to describe the value of receiving the Holy Spirit into our lives.

God's word, of course, says it much better than I. He tells us the fruits (that which is produced) of the indwelling of the Holy Spirit are as follows: **love, joy, peace, patience, kindness, goodness, faithfulness, gentleness, and self-control** (Galatians 5:22).

Aren't these the fruits we want to produce? Better yet, aren't these the fruits we wish everyone in our sphere of friends and family, our business owners, our teachers, our medical professionals, and our politicians produced? What if everyone in the world was indwelt with the Holy Spirit? I guess that would be heaven on earth, wouldn't it? We can only imagine. There will always be sin in this world. In fact, we don't stop sinning once we become believers, but we have that voice inside us to reveal the truth to us about what we're doing or about to do. If we are attentive to His voice, we will deal with the strong conviction He places in our hearts to help us avoid our sinful thoughts or actions. That's what a loving Father does.

I liken this brief human experience we're having to boot camp, a time of preparation for the eventual sinless life without end. This fallen world we occupy has been infiltrated with the spiritual forces of evil, which tainted the blood of mankind since the Garden of Eden. God says, *The life is in the blood*, Leviticus 17:11. Surely, we can all agree on that, right? Ponder this: *There is no forgiveness of sin without the shedding of blood* (Hebrews 9:22). So, the substance that gives and maintains life, our most valuable bodily component, blood, is the only thing our creator will accept as a worthy sacrifice in order to reach His Throne of Grace. Before Jesus was born into this world, God required animal blood sacrifices for atonement. But of course, God made a new covenant with mankind, allowing Jesus to serve as the **final** blood sacrifice necessary for forgiveness of sin – our sacrificial lamb. John the Baptist, a man who knew that his mission in this world was to prepare the way for the Lord (Matthew 3:3), appropriately introduced Jesus to the crowd: *Behold, the Lamb of God who takes away the sin of the world* (John 1:29). If we can simplify the role of Jesus, that introduction says it all; He shed His blood in our place. Thank you, Jesus! Though I'll never fully comprehend the blood concept this side of Heaven, I now understand as much about it as I need to know. But before I accessed my gift of the Holy Spirit, it made no sense at all, or one might say it was *foolishness* as we discovered earlier in 1 Corinthians 2:14. For those of you still questioning why God would establish an economy based on blood, let me just remind you that He is our creator. He makes the rules.

We Are Made to Commune with God – Not to Question His Authority!

He says we are to walk by faith, not by sight (2 Corinthians 5:7). He knows our finite minds cannot comprehend His thoughts or His ways (Isaiah 55:9). Isn't the fact that we are incapable of fully understanding God's ways reason enough to believe there is an omnipotent master, or at least someone smarter than the smartest human?

Jesus was not an afterthought, and the mandate of the blood sacrifice for atonement of sin was not an afterthought. Jesus's sacrifice is foretold from the beginning of His Word in Genesis. Let's just accept it and be thankful for it. He didn't wipe out sin; we still have free will. And in more than two thousand years since the birth of Jesus, man's sin continues to escalate beyond our imagination. Is it because mental illness has become rampant? Is it due to climate change?

In March 2023, our nation was once again caught off guard by a mass shooter, this time in a Nashville, Tennessee Christian school. The news reports constantly suggested this person must be mentally ill or emotionally disturbed. Now, seven months later, the officials have yet to release the manifesto of the killer (reported to be a Gen Z trans-sexual). Please keep in mind, the spiritual forces of evil will always resist the truth and will always seek cover of darkness. May I suggest something very few people dare to inject into this, or any other heinous crime story?

It's a Spiritual Issue!

How do we solve the crime issue in this country? I guess we could start by confiscating every gun from every gun owner, or better yet, confiscating only from those deemed to be an enemy of the state. We should start with Christian males who like to hunt; they've become culturally acceptable targets. We could pay for security guards (without guns, of course!) at every entrance to every school, church, store, restaurant, etc., but that would leave the sidewalks and streets un-manned. How can we stop the thugs who stroll by old people and beat them in the head for the fun of it, or how can we stop a maniacal driver from mowing down innocent people on sidewalks, or careening through a parade to kill as many people as possible? How can we stop terrorists from bombing our offices and places of worship? How can we stop mobs from violently invading retail stores, as they terrorize the employees and ransack the store to take as much merchandise as they can carry? How can we stop deadly drugs from getting into the hands of our children? How can we keep our children from becoming sex slaves, or keep their lives from being destroyed by evil forces who convince them they were born the wrong gender?

We can continue to put BAND-AIDS on the cancer, and wring our hands wondering what went wrong, or we can get to the root of the sickness and open our minds to the truth – not *my* truth, not *your* truth, but *THE* truth. Lies and misunderstandings keep us in bondage!

Knowing the Truth Sets Us Free! (John 8:32)

Here's the truth:

We have allowed the evil forces (spirits) of this world to overwhelm us. We, as a society, are not equipped to confront it. Here's why: We have removed our creator, our sustainer, our savior, and the source of wisdom from our lives, which has snow-balled into the removal of God's principles from our institutions – the foundations that sustain a society. Please consider this word from God:

> For our struggle is not against flesh and blood, but against the rulers, against the authorities, against the powers of this dark world, and against the spiritual forces of evil in the heavenly realms.
>
> Ephesians 6:12-13 (NIV)

There's that word again – spirit. Yes, there is a spiritual realm of evil that grows stronger by the day – so strong, in fact, that we've even elected government officials who are not only enabling evil behavior, but rewarding it, through cashless bail, defunding and demoralizing police, allowing the godless society of China to infiltrate our institutions of learning, and so much more. But let's remember, our battle is not against the individuals who espouse the deceitful lovely-sounding words of the day, but against the evil spiritual powers influencing this dark world. These officials making the bad decisions and incessantly lying to us are the instruments, not the maestro. I recall one of our leaders saying he would fundamentally transform America. When I heard that statement, I knew we were in trouble. What's wrong with the fundamentals of this nation, like *Life, liberty, and the pursuit of happiness,* or *One nation under God,* or *Equal justice under the Law*?

Those are fundamentals ordained by God Almighty from the beginning of this nation.

It's a Spiritual Issue!

How do we solve the crime issue in this country? I guess we could start by confiscating every gun from every gun owner, or better yet, confiscating only from those deemed to be an enemy of the state. We should start with Christian males who like to hunt; they've become culturally acceptable targets. We could pay for security guards (without guns, of course!) at every entrance to every school, church, store, restaurant, etc., but that would leave the sidewalks and streets un-manned. How can we stop the thugs who stroll by old people and beat them in the head for the fun of it, or how can we stop a maniacal driver from mowing down innocent people on sidewalks, or careening through a parade to kill as many people as possible? How can we stop terrorists from bombing our offices and places of worship? How can we stop mobs from violently invading retail stores, as they terrorize the employees and ransack the store to take as much merchandise as they can carry? How can we stop deadly drugs from getting into the hands of our children? How can we keep our children from becoming sex slaves, or keep their lives from being destroyed by evil forces who convince them they were born the wrong gender?

We can continue to put BAND-AIDS on the cancer, and wring our hands wondering what went wrong, or we can get to the root of the sickness and open our minds to the truth – not *my* truth, not *your* truth, but *THE* truth. Lies and misunderstandings keep us in bondage!

Knowing the Truth Sets Us Free!
(John 8:32)

Here's the truth:

We have allowed the evil forces (spirits) of this world to overwhelm us. We, as a society, are not equipped to confront it. Here's why: We have removed our creator, our sustainer, our savior, and the source of wisdom from our lives, which has snow-balled into the removal of God's principles from our institutions – the foundations that sustain a society. Please consider this word from God:

For our struggle is not against flesh and blood, but against the rulers, against the authorities, against the powers of this dark world, and against the spiritual forces of evil in the heavenly realms.

Ephesians 6:12-13 (NIV)

There's that word again – spirit. Yes, there is a spiritual realm of evil that grows stronger by the day – so strong, in fact, that we've even elected government officials who are not only enabling evil behavior, but rewarding it, through cashless bail, defunding and demoralizing police, allowing the godless society of China to infiltrate our institutions of learning, and so much more. But let's remember, our battle is not against the individuals who espouse the deceitful lovely-sounding words of the day, but against the evil spiritual powers influencing this dark world. These officials making the bad decisions and incessantly lying to us are the instruments, not the maestro. I recall one of our leaders saying he would fundamentally transform America. When I heard that statement, I knew we were in trouble. What's wrong with the fundamentals of this nation, like *Life, liberty, and the pursuit of happiness*, or *One nation under God*, or *Equal justice under the Law*?

Those are fundamentals ordained by God Almighty from the beginning of this nation.

How do we battle these spiritual forces of evil?

God tells us how to do it in Ephesians 6:13-17 (NIV):

Therefore, put on the full armor of God, so that when the day of evil comes, you may be able to stand your ground, and after you have done everything to stand. Stand firm then, with the belt of truth buckled around your waist, with the breastplate of righteousness in place, and with your feet fitted with the readiness that comes from the gospel of peace. In addition to all this, take up the shield of faith, with which you can extinguish all the flaming arrows of the evil one. Take the helmet of salvation and the sword of the Spirit which is the word of God.

Imagine if you will, the armor worn by a Roman soldier. I hope you will come to appreciate how God meets us where we are to help us understand His will for His people. Certainly, the audience of circa 60 AD could relate to the soldier's armor as God reveals it to the Apostle Paul. And of course, we too can understand it, having the benefit of historical evidence. I find it interesting to note that the Apostle Paul warns us to *stand firm* three times (Ephesians 6:11, 13, 14) leading up to his explanation of the Armor of God. I think our take-away from that should be that we are not to be appeasing, mushy wimps when we're confronted by evil, but we are to stand our ground, through the power of the Holy Spirit. It has been made clear to me that we sinful creatures cannot fight the battle in our own strength. The believer is equipped with all the right tools to do battle. Let's briefly examine our defensive and offensive weapons as explained through the beautiful analogy of the Roman soldier's armor:

Belt of Truth

Buckling the belt of truth around your waist (aka - girding your loins) was paramount for the Roman soldier when preparing for battle. They wore a loose-fitting tunic that would certainly encumber them in battle, so the good soldier would pull up the loose ends of his tunic and tuck them into his belt.[4] This analogy tells me we can't begin our battle without first getting rid of the annoyances that hinder us from the truth. Truth is the baseline from which all battles should be fought, and for that matter on which all decisions should be made. What are some annoyances or hindrances that keep us from acting or speaking from a position of truth in the 21st century?

Believing everything we see on social media is a big one! We need to be on guard at all times for lies that are taught to us and our children. Parents, when we turn over our most important job in this life, child-rearing, to our electronic devices, we relinquish the education, the social development, and the spiritual development of our precious little ones to Satan, the father of lies. I know that seems harsh, but somebody's got to say it! We've got to put away the cell phones in order to raise well-rounded, thoughtful, independent thinkers (And God only knows the damage these electronic devices do to young, developing brains). Let's use our devices as tools of efficiency, not our very identity, and certainly not as baby-sitters. Let children develop their personalities through authentic human interaction. They do what they see us doing!

I remember when the news could be trusted because reporters lived by a code of ethics that mandated they be seekers and purveyors of truth regardless how they felt personally about the person or topic making the news. Those days are gone, but God's Word stands forever (Isaiah 40:8). And we who have taken hold of the Holy Spirit in our lives are equipped to discern truth from lies. Gird your loins with this truth from the spoken word of Jesus:

If you love me, you will obey what I command. And I will ask the Father, and he will give you another Counselor to be with you forever – the Spirit of Truth [The Holy Spirit].
The world cannot accept him, because it neither sees him nor knows him. But you know him, for he lives with you and will be in you.

John 14:15-17 (NIV)

BREASTPLATE OF RIGHTEOUSNESS

The Roman soldier's breastplate would be made of tough leather, with animal horn or hoof pieces sewn on, covering the torso to protect the heart and vital organs.[4] The Lord takes care of the righteous. The Holy Spirit drew me to Genesis 6:9 - *Noah was a righteous man, blameless among the people of his time, and he walked with God.* That makes it clear to me that God honors righteousness, protects righteousness, and uses the righteous man or woman to achieve great things in battle. We can only imagine how many arrows of ridicule and scorn Noah's breastplate of righteousness repelled as he powered through his seemingly impossible assignment.

FEET FITTED WITH THE READINESS THAT COMES FROM THE GOSPEL OF PEACE

Roman soldiers wore boots with nails in them to grip the ground in battle.[4] In their hand-to-hand combat, the death blow would surely come if they got knocked off their feet. Planting our feet in readiness to battle the evil one requires confidence in peace through strength. We get that confidence/readiness through prayer and trust in God. It's beyond our understanding, but it's there for the asking. Philippians 4:6-7 tells us:

> *Do not be anxious about anything, but in everything, by prayer and petition, with thanksgiving, present your requests to God. And the peace of God, which transcends all* [human] *understanding, will guard your hearts and your minds in Christ Jesus.*

Shield of Faith

The shield protects the entire body. We must believe in our cause through faith if we are to deflect the flaming temptations of the evil one. In fact, God is our shield. In Psalm 18, David, the young man anointed to be King of Israel, sang to the Lord after being delivered from his enemies. Verse 30 says: *As for God, his way is perfect; the word of the Lord is flawless. He is a shield for all who take refuge in him.*

Helmet of Salvation

Paul is referring to the believer, those who have accepted the gift of salvation through Jesus Christ. The non-believer obviously doesn't have access to the helmet of salvation. The head is the primary target for Satan. He challenges what we believe to be true and he makes us question or doubt our knowledge of God's Word - hence, the need for protection against the arrows intended to cause us to doubt our salvation. The gift of salvation comes with a bonus – protection of the mind against lies and futile thinking.

Sword of the Spirit

What is the Sword of the Spirit? The only offensive weapon in our arsenal against the evil one – The Sword of the Spirit is the infallible, incorruptible, holy Word of God. *All scripture is God-breathed and useful for teaching, rebuking, correcting, and training in righteousness* (2 Timothy 3:16). *It* [God's Word] *is living and active. Sharper than any double-edged sword ...* (Hebrews 4:12). Written through prophets and eye witnesses as communicated by the Spirit of God, it is spiritually discerned by those seeking Him in Spirit and in Truth (John 4:24).

The Bible has been protected through centuries to become the bestselling book of all time. Research conducted by the British and Foreign Bible Society in 2021 suggests that the total number sold probably lies between five and seven billion copies.[5]

Let's stop for a moment and ponder the absurdity and unadulterated evil of a culture who would declare that the best-selling book of all time, the book that the culture's laws and lifestyle were built upon, should suddenly and permanently be outlawed as a teaching tool, and even as a visible historical document, in our institutions of learning. Please take heed, friends; this is just one of the diabolical schemes intended to erase a culture.

In light of that truth alone, it becomes crystal clear why we need the full armor of God. We believers have just rolled over in battle. And this is what we get – two generations of a moth-eaten armor with no sword in sight. And we are suffering mightily for it. God's Word is not lofty theories; it is written for our safety, security, and happiness. It's high time we say *Thank you*, pay attention, and do what it says! In other words, *Be doers of the Word, and not hearers only, deceiving yourselves* (James 1:22, ESV).

I was raised during the Cold War with the USSR (Union of Soviet Socialist Republics). It was an atheistic, socialist culture.

Ronald Reagan referred to it as The Evil Empire for good reason. It's hard for me to believe we have elected politicians today who proudly claim to be socialists. I wonder if they really know what it means to be a socialist. The trend to re-write history could be the reason for our collective ignorance on the subject.

Now that we've lost so many battles for the minds and souls of our children, it's going to take a courageous army to wage a new war to reclaim that which we cowardly gave away to the enemy. The war can be won with a single non-violent weapon – *The Sword of the Spirit which is The Word of God.*

In preparation for the war, please stay with me to investigate and learn from Satan's victories from the Garden of Eden to the U.S. Supreme Court and beyond. An effective soldier conducts reconnaissance before making a battle plan. In other words, as unpleasant as it is, we need to know our enemy.

Chapter 2

The Evil Spirit

There is another spirit - the evil one known as Satan, the devil, Lucifer, Beelzebub, and other names. He is alive and well and wreaking havoc on earth. The crimes, the injustices, the ignorance, the inclination to believe lies over truth, and the ever-present chaos are just a few of the signs of his endeavors. If you don't believe he exists among us, just take a look in any of our major cities at the sheer depravity, and the zombie-like shells of human beings wandering the streets.

We don't hear much talk about Satan or hell, do we? There's a reason for that. We don't want to be canceled because those topics are unpleasant to think about, and it would be bullying to suggest some people are hell-bound, right? So, we just don't bring it up. Even our pastors seem to steer clear of the subject. I do not profess to be an expert on Satan, but I can certainly see the results of his presence in our world, and witness the prolific surge of his power. Let's face it; his power is real. If you watch trustworthy news at all, you can plainly see that we're moving closer to hell on earth every day. I prayed as to whether I should broach the topic of Satan, and as usual, the Lord drew me to His *Sword of the Spirit* to teach me, and equip me to share with you what I've learned. I trust He is revealing all we need to know at this point in time, within the confines of our limited understanding. I will rely on the words of Proverbs 3:5-6:

Trust in the Lord with all your heart and do not lean on your own understanding. In all your ways acknowledge Him, and He will make your paths straight.

My Prayer: I'm acknowledging you, Lord. Please show me what you want me to reveal about our enemy. I want to be a conduit for your word. Guard my spirit and my mind to write only what is true and ordained by your hand. I trust you with all my heart to direct my path.

God gives the following word to His prophet Ezekiel regarding the creation and fall of Satan:

> *You were in Eden, the garden of God;*
> *Every precious stone was your covering:*
> *The ruby, the topaz and the diamond;*
> *The beryl, the onyx and the jasper;*
> *The lapis lazuli, the turquoise and the emerald:*
> *And the gold, the workmanship of your settings and sockets,*
> *was in you. On the day you were created they were prepared.*
> *You were the anointed cherub, who covers,*
> *and I placed you there. You were on the holy mountain of God;*
> *You walked in the midst of the stones of fire.*
> *You were blameless in your ways from the day you were created*
> *Until unrighteousness was found in you*
> *so I banished you in disgrace from the mountain of God.*
> *I expelled you, O mighty guardian, from your place among the stones of fire. Your heart was filled with pride because of all your beauty. Your wisdom was corrupted by your love of splendor.*
> *So I threw you to the ground.*

Ezekiel 28:13-17 (NIV)

Lucifer (meaning Shining One) was created as a beautiful angelic creature, ordained as the mighty guardian cherub. But Lucifer was given free will just as humans, and note how he used his free will – to elevate himself above his creator. Notice all his *I wills* in the following passage from God's word.

> *How you have fallen from heaven,*
> *morning star, son of the dawn!*
> *You have been cast down to the earth,*
> *you who once laid low the nations!*
> *You said in your heart, 'I will ascend to the heavens;*
> *I will raise my throne above the stars of God;*
> *I will sit enthroned on the mount of assembly,*
> *on the utmost heights of the sacred mountain.*
> *I will ascend above the tops of the clouds;*
> *I will make myself like the Most High.*
>
> Isaiah 14:12-14 (NIV)

In summary, *Pride goeth before a fall!* Let's see what God's word says about pride:

> *Pride goes before destruction,*
> *And a haughty spirit before a fall.*
> *It is better to be humble in spirit with the lowly*
> *Than to divide the spoil with the proud.*
> *He who gives attention to the word will find good,*
> *And blessed is he who trusts in the Lord.*
>
> Proverbs 16:18-20 (NASB)

God threw Lucifer out of Heaven to Earth, where he torments mankind, and will do so until the end of earth as we know it. Satan will ultimately be thrown into the lake of fire for eternity (Revelation 20:10), while we who trust in the Lord will enjoy life everlasting, free from Satan, but safe in the loving arms of God Almighty. Can I get an Amen!

Now back to earth – While we're here we must learn to battle the evil one. In order to do that, we need to learn Satan's typical strategy. He chooses language that sounds lovely, and simultaneously caters to our selfish, carnal desires, such as fame, being liked or admired, being prideful (which he knows so well!) or our inclination toward laziness. He also thrives in ignorance, which is why it's so important to him to keep our children ignorant of the Word of God. There are innumerable insecurities and sins of all stripes that are always ripe for picking in every human. Satan, like any thief, chooses our most vulnerable point of entry. Let's get a glimpse of Satan's method of operation as outlined in the infallible Sword of the Spirit. But I want to make clear that the born again believer is not vulnerable to possession by the devil. However, we are fair game to him when it comes to interference in our lives. That's why we need to guard ourselves with the full armor of God.

In the Garden of Eden, God gives explicit instructions to Adam, which Adam then conveys to Eve: *You are free to eat from any tree in the garden; but you must not eat from the tree of the knowledge of good and evil, for when you eat of it you will surely die* Genesis 2:16b-17.

Satan approaches Eve with a question: *Has God said, 'You shall not eat from any tree of the garden?'* Eve responds with the instructions from God. The consequences were clearly understood; they would surely die if they ate from the one tree of knowledge of good and evil.

Satan: *You surely will not die! For God knows that in the day you eat from it your eyes will be opened, and you will be like God, knowing good and evil* Genesis 3:4-5.

We know that the serpent (Satan) is cunning and attractive, and he exudes confidence and authority (then and now!). Eve was seduced. She didn't display a motive of anger toward God, but reasoned in her limited knowledge that the serpent must be smarter than she or God. She reasoned that the tree was good for food, [What could be wrong with food? Why would God put it here if he didn't want us to eat it?], and that it was a delight to the eyes [It's too beautiful to be harmful] and that the tree was desirable to make one wise [Why shouldn't I be wise? Surely, I misunderstood God, or is the serpent correct; God is jealous that I would be as knowledgeable as He?]. She took some and ate it. Also, she gave some to her mate, [Just in case God's right, I'm not going down alone! Misery does love company after all].

Enter sin. Enter death. Enter pain and suffering. But Adam and Eve got what they wanted, knowledge of good and evil. They suddenly gained the knowledge that they were naked! Innocence was replaced with guilt and shame.

The Bottom Line is – Satan Distorts Truth – Then and Now!

Eve wasn't blatantly rebellious. She was duped. She reasoned away her actions of disobedience. She didn't have on the full armor of God! I know the *armor* wasn't articulated until centuries later; however she certainly had the word of God clearly telling her not to eat from the tree of knowledge of good and evil. God even made clear the consequence of the sin – death. Death wasn't part of God's perfect creation; sin created it. But God, in His unfathomable love for us, gave us a way out. He would come to earth in the form of a baby born of a virgin to be the perfect sacrificial lamb to redeem us from our sin. He didn't create us to throw us away; He created us to love us and commune with us. Psalm 100:5 reminds us:

For the Lord is good; His mercy is everlasting; and His truth endures to all generations.

I like to use the easy-to-remember definitions of Mercy and Grace:

Mercy is withholding the punishment we deserve.

Grace is unmerited favor or giving us what we don't deserve.

My Prayer: Thank you, Lord that your mercy is everlasting. You know I need it daily and your word tells us your mercy is new every morning.

I memorized the 100th Psalm as a six-year-old in Vacation Bible School. I'm reminded of another scripture I learned as a child: *My word will not return void* (Isaiah 55:11). Even though I didn't understand the meaning of either of those scriptures as a child, God didn't allow the words to leave me. His Word is always there when I need it and it always meets me where I am at the time I need it. That's just a miracle of The *Sword of the Spirit*. It cannot be witnessed from afar; it must be experienced. I want everyone to experience it! But for those of you thinking the word of God is just ancient myths, please ponder, once again, this truth found in Hebrews 4:12: *The word of God is living and active and sharper than any two-edged sword, and piercing as far as the division of soul and spirit, of both joints and marrow, and able to judge the thoughts and intentions of the heart.*

When Adam and Eve fell to the wiles of Satan, the blood of mankind was tainted forever with the propensity to sin. What is sin? Sin is disobeying God, or putting ourselves or anything else before Him. God will not engage with sin (Remember: His creation; His rules). Sin separates us from Him. Before you say, *That's not fair!* or *If he was a loving God, why would He let us sin, or let bad things happen to us,* or better still – *why did He create Satan,* or ..., let's keep in mind, God created mankind for the purpose of fellowship with us. He wants our companionship! And our job is simply to glorify Him in our good works. By the way, the term *fair* as it relates to our worldly definition of fairness is not found in the scriptures. Also, God did not create us like robots. That's a human creation which can be used for good or evil, just like money, guns, businesses, or anything else created by mankind.

God created us with souls to live eternally, spirits to allow communication/fellowship with Him, and a FREE WILL in order to choose our path, to set goals, to learn, to achieve, to have empathy, to discern right and wrong, to give and receive love, and to accept or reject Him.

Now let's fast forward to another blatant attempt by Satan to tempt none other than the Son of God. Jesus had just been baptized by His relative, John the Baptist (another miraculous birth and divine orchestration of God's perfect plan found in Luke 1:5-25). Jesus prepared to begin His ministry by following the leading of The Holy Spirit into the wilderness, where He would fast for forty days. Jesus, being fully God, yet fully man, would undoubtedly be hungry after forty days. Enter Satan. Remember, he always tempts us where we're most vulnerable. For us, it might be through our desire to be liked, or respected, or admired, or any other selfish vulnerability. For Jesus, it was His hunger. Satan said to Jesus, *If you are the Son of God, command that these stones become bread* Matthew 4:3.

How does Jesus respond? He uses His offensive weapon in the armor of God – The Sword of the Spirit, which is the Word of God!

Jesus replies with Old Testament truth: *It is written, 'Man shall not live on bread alone, but on every word that proceeds out of the mouth of God'* (Deuteronomy 8:3).

After Satan's first attempt fails, he goes for a second temptation. This time he thinks he can get to Jesus through the human desire for power and prominence. His tactic is to try the same thing he did with Eve – twist the truth of God's Word.

Then the devil took Him into the holy city and had Him stand on the pinnacle of the temple, and said to Him, 'If you are the Son of God, throw yourself down; for it is written [in Psalms 91:11-12], *He will command His angels concerning You, and on their hands they will bear You up, so that You will not strike Your foot against a stone'*

Matthew 4:5-6

Jesus draws His sword of the spirit again, quoting Old Testament prophecy: *Jesus said to him, 'On the other hand, it is written* [in Deuteronomy 6:16], *you shall not put the Lord your God to the test'*

Matthew 4:7

Now Satan makes a third attempt to trick the Son of God:

Again, the devil took Him to a very high mountain and showed Him all the kingdoms of the world and their glory; and he said to Him, 'All these things I will give You, if You fall down and worship me.' Then Jesus said to him, 'Go, Satan! For it is written, you shall worship the Lord your God, and serve Him only.' Then the devil left Him and behold, angels came and began to minister to Him.

Matthew 4:8-11

Don't be deceived; the spirit of Satan is alive and well in our world today. The Apostle Peter warns: *Be of sober spirit, be on the alert. Your adversary, the devil, prowls around like a roaring lion, seeking someone to devour* 1 Peter 5:8.

How many people of prominence do you know today who have been devoured by the evil one? Let's keep emotions out of it; avoid thinking of someone you simply dislike, or someone who has opposing political views; just think about someone whom you know for a fact distorted or ignored the truth to promote a lie (Could *you* be one of them?). These people range from social media influencers, to so-called journalists, to educators, to the highest officials in government, to jealous co-workers, or even jealous family members. Satan uses them to twist truth, just as he did successfully with Eve, and unsuccessfully with Jesus. Our very lexicon has been twisted and perverted to turn pleasant, harmless words and phrases into tools of Satan, a means to dupe the vulnerable (i.e. those without the indwelling of the Holy Spirit).

Here are just a few of the words or phrases used in our public discourse today that *sound* righteous, but are quite the opposite – Satan's modus operandi:

Women's Healthcare –
Code for abortion

Pro-Choice –
Code for condoning the killing of babies in the womb

Choice has become a positive word unless it means choosing to do the righteous thing, or choosing to think independently. Why is *choice* not allowed for a mother who chooses life for her child, and seeks services from a pregnancy help center? Our satanic culture says it's okay to destroy, defame, or intimidate those women, as well as those who attempt to help them. There are many who would step out in traffic to save an animal, but condone killing a human infant, not only in the womb, but even after birth. That, my friend, is the influence of Satan himself!

I don't want to seem insensitive to the difficulty some women endure in their decision to end their baby's life. But may I suggest there are just some decisions we shouldn't agonize over, and taking a life for our comfort is one such decision. God's Word is very clear on this.

I've never been faced with the decision of abortion, but I can look back on other decisions I made as an immature Christian, remembering how I agonized over them, wondering what to do, when in more mature hindsight, I now wonder why I was twisting myself in knots over those decisions when God's answer was staring me in the face all along.

I know several women who will always live with great remorse following the decision to end their baby's life. Those women are now committed to spending the rest of their lives helping other women avoid the consequences they've endured. I acknowledge that pregnancies resulting from rape are certainly a heavier burden, but God is able to work that out too. Please trust that anything people mean for evil, God can use for good (Genesis 50:20). And ...*God causes all things to work together for good to those who love God, to those who are called according to His purpose* (Romans 8:28).

I'm not preaching as one who claims to have never sinned; I'm speaking to you as one sinner to another. We ALL sin! *All sin and fall short of the glory of God* (Romans 3:23). In fact, Jesus points out that hating someone is spiritually the same as murder: *Everyone who hates his brother is a murderer* (1 John 3:15). Abortion just happens to be a sin the world is condoning, and even celebrating at our peril, and it must be addressed honestly. I think it's fair to say the vast majority of unwanted pregnancies result from consensual relations. Young women, please understand *choice* doesn't begin *after* the pregnancy; choice is available to women *before* the pregnancy. But the young girls marching with signs saying, *My Body; My Choice* don't seem willing to acknowledge that they ignore their right to *choose* to get pregnant in the first place, and they don't seem to consider that abortion is not destroying *their* body; it's destroying *someone else's* body by choice – perhaps to satisfy their own comfort, convenience, vanity, fear, hate, or some other self-serving reason. Wouldn't that be the very definition of murder? I've never heard a politician or even the staunchest pro-lifer use the 'M' word when talking about abortion, even the after-birth abortions. I wonder why.

Giving yourself to another in the most intimate way known to humankind is a choice. If you find it was a bad choice, death is not going to correct it. Covering one sin with another is never the answer.

Now, if you are faced with an unwanted pregnancy and you don't have the indwelling of the Holy Spirit to guide and equip you, stop here and receive the answer that will set you free!

Confess to God that you are a sinner. Tell Him you acknowledge that He sent Jesus to take your punishment – death. *The wages of sin is death, but the free gift of God is eternal life in Christ Jesus our Lord* (Romans 6:23). Thank Him for your free gift. Acknowledge that He was raised from the dead and sent the Holy Spirit to be His presence with you now and forever. Ask Him to come into your life and guide you to do His will. Repent (turn) from your sin. Then do what the Holy Spirit leads you to do. He'll speak to you through His Word (the Bible), through other mature believers, and through circumstances to help you make the right choices. You're not condemned!

Therefore there is now no condemnation for those who are in Christ Jesus. For the law of the Spirit of life in Christ Jesus has set you free from the law of sin and of death.

Romans 8:1-2 (NASB)

Before I leave the *Pro-Choice* issue, I have to be obedient to the Holy Spirit's leading. As I moved on to the next topic, the Lord led me back to this one to say this:

Partial Obedience = 100% Disobedience

I am reminded that God answered fifty years of the fervent prayers of His people to reverse Roe v. Wade, the scourge on our nation that has killed more than 42,521,000 babies between 1973 and 2020. [6]

Are we going to respond to this answered prayer with partial obedience? Is 15 weeks the right number to kill a baby, or is it 6 weeks, or when we hear the heartbeat, or when the baby feels pain, or is it just whatever is right in our own eyes?

Gender Affirming Care–
Code for the opposite of gender affirmation –
gender destruction

I ask those over thirty-five years of age, could you have ever imagined that our government would condone the mutilation of children's bodies, minds and spirits by attempting to change their gender, and boldly doing so while hiding it from the child's parents? We have just begun to witness the wiles of Satan. We're moving closer to hell on earth every day; that's why we need to access the full armor of God!

As one who has taught children for over thirty-five years, I can tell you they have no concept of right or wrong as it relates to their sexual image. Give me a break! Kids who believe in Santa Claus, the Tooth Fairy, and the Easter Bunny are hardly equipped to understand the consequences of changing their very identity! A little girl might say she wants to be a boy for various reasons. Perhaps she likes to play what they play, and relates with the things they do or say. But she does not understand sex! They don't understand the forever consequences of damaging the divine balance of their physiology. Young children believe whatever they are told. They are literal thinkers. This truth was never more perfectly demonstrated to me than when I saw a video in which a parent was tossing a ball to his little girl as she held the ball bat. *Keep your eye on the ball*, he instructed. The child dutifully bent over to literally touch her eye to the ball where it lay on the ground!

Consider the adolescent. What adolescent have you ever known who wasn't confused about sex? What adolescent doesn't feel insecure about his or her body? Now raise these kids to become addicted to social media, where they take counsel from other confused kids 24 hours a day. What do you get? A toxic fad to help them wallow in their shared insecurities – gender change!

Again, let me interject here that I don't profess to be an expert, but then again, WHO IS? I contend there can be no expert in the changing of a person's gender! If there was ever a time to accuse someone of playing God, gender change is such a time! I have to wonder if the medical *professionals* engaging in this behavior aren't quietly seeing each case with a slight sense of scientific experimentation. They do their deeds and move on to make big paychecks and make big names for themselves, perhaps vying for Nobel prizes, while leaving behind the children who suffer all kinds of emotional, physical, relational, and yes, spiritual devastation for the rest of their lives. Children know NOT what they do! That's why God designed the family with parents to lead them and teach them right from wrong. Unfortunately, we have a parenting crisis in this country. And those parents who try to *stand firm against the schemes of the evil one* (Ephesians 6:11) are often vilified and ostracized by the evil influencers. Please consider this warning from God regarding those who would influence children to sin:

> *And whoever receives one such child in My name receives Me; but whoever causes one of these little ones who believe in Me to stumble, it would be better for him to have a heavy millstone hung around his neck, and to be drowned in the depth of the sea (Matthew 18: 5-6).*

God takes this seriously and we should too. Children are not meant to be experimental subjects at the hands of self-serving adults. I'll shout a big AMEN to the *millstone* approach for anyone who would take advantage of a child's malleable mind, causing him or her to be outside the will of God! And I can say with 100% certainty that it is not God's will to re-assign the gender He ordained!

God Does Not Make Mistakes!

I taught sixth grade girls in Sunday school for several years. During the Boy Band craze of the 90's, I was trying to make the point with them how unreliable our emotions can be. I asked them to name their favorite boy band; they were very animated in their gushing love for one band in particular. They're also group-thinkers at that age (Some of us never advance past the group-think stage!) Then, I asked them how they felt about a particular boy band that I knew was extremely popular just one year prior. When I mentioned this band's name, they were very animated again, but with Boooos and thumbs down. Just a year ago, these same girls couldn't get enough of the same group they're now booing with great passion. I tried to use this as an example of how our emotions can change so drastically and quickly at their age.

What makes us think the adolescent mind is equipped to decide to change his or her gender for life? I wonder if anyone ever counsels potential *transkids* that they are making a decision to never produce children of their own. Many adults struggle with that question; how can we expect adolescents to make that decision? Hasn't the religion of science declared that the frontal lobe (the decision-making part) of the human brain isn't fully developed until the approximate age of twenty-five? How can one follow that accepted science, while advocating the acceptance of a child's decision to change his or her gender? A divided mind is fertile ground for Satan.

I am reminded of the Nazi physician, Josef Mengele, who mutilated captive Jews in the name of scientific research. Most of his subjects were children. It is just too horrifying to list his experiments, but I think it should be noted that one of his endeavors was to attempt sex change operations.[7] History has rightfully branded him an evil man, yet twenty-first century doctors, who mutilate children, are lauded, protected, and paid handsomely.

Climate Change –
Formerly known as *Global Warming*

The term, global warming, didn't work long term since the earth wasn't warming enough to strike fear in independent thinkers. On the other hand, it's hard to deny that climate does change, thus enabling the gullible to throw that term around without having to subject themselves to meaningful debate. I am fully onboard with being a good steward of the earth. In fact, God tells us we are to *fill the earth, subdue it, rule over the fish of the sea, the birds of the air, and over every living thing that moves on the earth* (Genesis 1:28). God put mankind in charge of the earth and the animals, but He didn't say that mankind could determine when the end of this world would take place. In fact, He makes it very clear that no one knows the day or time (Matthew 24:36). I heard an ignorant, immature, self-righteous politician tell us that the world would end in twelve years, unless we do what he or she tells us to do. Could a human be more ill-informed and self-righteous? Talk about playing God!

I find it interesting that all four of the above perverted terms have a common theme – they all deny God's creation and His omnipotence. I'm blown away by the audacity of those who actually believe mankind can move the earth's date of destruction, or change when life begins, or decide when children need to have their very gender changed, while denying the creation of the family and autonomy of parents.

These spiritually empty vessels who promote these abominations have esteemed themselves above the only One who can control the earth, the One who spoke it into being. That, my friends, is a scheme of Satan. He has infiltrated their minds with futile thoughts of superiority over God, just like he did with Eve (Remember Satan's goals articulated in Isaiah 14:13-14). These people have obviously not accessed the Holy Spirit, therefore they are not able to put on the full armor of God in order to stand firm against the schemes of the devil.

If you don't believe me, please consider how divisive and destructive these ideas have been to our nation. When precepts are righteous (God-centered), they are never destructive to peace; they are never destructive to mental health, and they are never destructive to the human body.

May I suggest three words for all of us to marinate in our spirits before making any future decisions, or making speeches, or posting on social media, etc.

Check Your Motives

Those three words would make all decisions much easier! I wish those words would become the mantra for all politicians and public servants. If they could just ask these questions:

Will my motives result in glorifying God, or am I looking for personal glory?

What is best for the people I serve?

Self-glorification results in failure, especially for those who have been hired to represent others. Appeasing someone for the purpose of being liked is never the right option; it doesn't work in rearing children, or in international diplomacy, or in politics. The irony of appeasement is that the appeaser is never respected by the one being appeased. Truth matters. It sets us free. Let's turn our CYA attitudes into CYM attitudes and remember to check our motives before every committee meeting, before every interview, before every debate, and before every vote. We'll truly make a difference for good and make huge strides in overcoming the unholy world.

If you can't honestly check your motives, perhaps you haven't received the indwelling of the Holy Spirit. Here's how to take care of that:

Ask the Holy Spirit to inhabit you through acceptance of the gift of salvation through Jesus, the virgin-born Son of God who came to be sacrificed for your atonement of sin. Tell someone about your decision. Romans 10:9 tells us: *If you confess with your mouth Jesus is Lord, and believe in your heart that God raised Him from the dead, you will be saved; for with the heart a person believes, resulting in righteousness, and with the mouth he confesses, resulting in salvation.*

I feel led of the Holy Spirit to share a 1965 radio broadcast that has proven to be prophetic. The author is Paul Harvey. If you have invited God to be Lord of your life, you possess the divine ability to ponder this speech through the discernment of the Holy Spirit. If you want to hear the iconic voice of Mr. Harvey, this speech can easily be found audibly.

If I Were the Devil...

If I were the prince of darkness, I'd want to engulf the whole world in darkness and I'd have one third of its real estate and four fifths of its population. But I wouldn't be happy until I had seized the ripest apple on the tree – Thee. So I'd set about however necessary to take over the United States [because it's founded *Under God*] I'd subvert the churches first. I'd begin with a campaign of whispers. With the wisdom of a serpent, I would whisper to you as I whispered to Eve *Do as you please*. To the young, I would whisper that the Bible is a myth. I would convince them that man created God instead of the other way around. I would confide that what's bad is good and what's good is "square." And the old, I would teach to pray after me: Our father, which art in Washington …

And then I'd get organized. I'd educate authors in how to make lurid literature exciting so that anything else would appear dull and uninteresting. I'd threaten TV with dirtier movies and vice versa. I'd pedal narcotics to whom I could. I'd sell alcohol to ladies and gentlemen of distinction. I'd tranquilize the rest with pills. If I were the devil, I'd soon have families at war with themselves. Churches at war with themselves. Nations at war with themselves until each in its turn was consumed. And with promises of higher ratings, I'd have mesmerizing media fanning the flames. If I were the devil, I would encourage schools to refine young intellects, but neglect to discipline emotions – just let these run wild! Until before you knew it, you'd have to have drug-sniffing dogs and metal detectors at every schoolhouse door. Within a decade, you'd have prisons overflowing. I'd have judges promoting pornography. Soon I'd evict God from the courthouse, then the schoolhouse. And then from the houses of congress. And in his own churches, I would substitute psychology for religion. And deify science. I would lure priests and pastors into misusing boys and girls and church money.

If I were the devil, I'd make the symbol of Easter an egg and the symbol of Christmas a bottle. If I were the devil, I'd take from those who have, and give to those who wanted until I had killed the incentive of the ambitious. And what do you bet I couldn't get whole states to promote gambling as the way to get rich. I would caution against extremes in hard work, in patriotism, in moral conduct. I would convince the young that marriage is old fashioned, that swinging is more fun, that what you see on TV is the way to be and thus I could undress you in public and I could lure you into bed with diseases for which there is no cure. In other words, if I were the devil, I'd just keep right on doing what he's doing.[8]

Chapter 3

Spirit on the Supreme Court

How did we get to this level of depravity and ignorance? Let's travel back to 1962 for one answer.

What is the phrase we've all been taught to explain why we can't pray or teach God's Word in our schools?

You guessed it – Separation of Church and State. We've been taught that's what the First Amendment to the Constitution says.

However...

Separation of Church and State appears in NO founding document of the United States of America. Of course, some might say even though those words aren't in the Constitution, that's still the intent of the First Amendment. Let's explore. What *is* the intent of the First Amendment?

To understand the intent of the First Amendment, we should look at the rough drafts penned by its author. I know if anyone wanted to know my intent on a topic, my rough drafts would certainly reveal it.

A congressman named Fisher Ames offered the wording for the First Amendment; please consider his drafts:

First Draft - Congress shall not make any law establishing any religious denomination.

Second Draft - Congress shall make no law establishing any particular denomination.

Third Draft - Congress shall make no law establishing any particular denomination in preference to others.

Final Draft - Congress shall make no law respecting an establishment of religion, or prohibiting the free exercise thereof. [9]

Did you see anything in there about *separation of church and state*? I didn't.

I think we can see in these drafts that the words religion and denomination were interchangeable in Ames's mind. Our founding fathers were Christian. Appeasing atheists was not in their thinking. They didn't want what they had experienced in Great Britain, one denomination ruling the government to the exclusion of all others. There are so many writings by the framers of the Constitution to prove that they would never accept the separation we've embraced today. In writing an article for a national magazine, Fisher Ames expressed his concerns that as more and more textbooks were introduced in the classroom, the Bible should not take a backseat to other textbooks. He wrote, *[Why] should not the Bible regain the place it once held as a school book? Its morals are pure; its examples captivating and noble. The reverence for the Sacred Book that is thus early impressed lasts long; and probably if not impressed in infancy, never takes firm hold of the mind.*[10]

Clearly, the use of the Bible in the classroom didn't offend Fisher Ames, and he's the one who authored the House language for the

First Amendment! He understood the importance of teaching God's Word to the young, just as God said: *Train a child in the way he should go, and when he is old he will not depart from it* Proverbs 22:6.

John Adams, signer of the Declaration of Independence and our second president, had these words to say about the Bible:

> *Suppose a nation in some distant region should take the Bible for their only law book and every member should regulate his conduct by the precepts there exhibited ... What a Eutopia, what a Paradise would this region be. I have examined all [religions] ... and the result is that the Bible is the best Book in the world.*[10]

For approximately 170 years, the First Amendment had meant a **federally established** denomination/religion. But the court, in 1962, allowed Satan to fashion a snowball that would pick up thousands of cases in its path, ultimately resulting in the banishment of God in the public classroom. Furthermore, any religious activity in public places has been deemed unconstitutional. God was officially removed from the public affairs of this nation founded *Under God*. So how did we get so separated from the original intent of the First Amendment? It goes back to a private letter Thomas Jefferson wrote to the Danbury, Connecticut Baptist Association. The Danbury Baptists had expressed concern that the Congregationalist denomination (or others) was planned to become the National Denomination. Jefferson answered them in a letter assuring them there was no basis for their fear because the free exercise of religion would never be interfered with by government. He told them that the First Amendment built a wall of separation between church and state.[11]

That, my friends, is an example of the spirit of evil (aka Satan) twisting truth once again! It strikes remarkable similarity to his tactics with Eve. Satan will take a benign statement, and contort it into something unrecognizable. I contend the members of multiple Supreme Courts did not access the full armor of God in order to stand firm. And we have suffered mightily for their failure!

Engel v. Vitale, 1962

The Board of Regents of the State of New York instituted a policy offering a prayer to be said at the beginning of every school day. The Board of Regents composed a non-sectarian prayer to be recited, and provided it to the school districts. Parents of students at one of the New York school districts sued, arguing that the prayer violated the First Amendment of the U.S. Constitution. This is the prayer in question:

Almighty God, we acknowledge our dependence upon thee, and we beg thy blessings upon us, our parents, our teachers, and our country. [12]

The school district argued that since the prayer was voluntary and non-sectarian, and since no student was punished for not participating, reciting the prayer was not an establishment of religion.

The petitioners argued that having state officials compose a prayer for students to recite at the beginning of a school day, even if it was voluntary, and the prayer was non-denominational, was a violation of the First Amendment's Establishment Clause.

Mr. Engel and a group of parents eventually won the Engel v. Vitale case. The Supreme Court of the United States overturned the rulings of three lower courts and determined that the prayer, even though voluntary and denominationally neutral, because it was composed by the Board of Regents, a state government body, violated the Establishment Clause of the First Amendment. [13]

Sadly, the Engel case has been cited in every subsequent prayer case since 1962, regardless of its dissimilarity to the New York case.[14] Consistent with his modus operandi, it seems Satan used this case to misconstrue the Engel decision to include any type of prayers in school, or any positive mention of God for that matter.

I find it so interesting that the court chooses not to cite the author of The First Amendment when deciding prayer cases. It only cites its own previous bad decisions and passes them off as original intent.

David Barton points out in his book, *Original Intent*, that when the court struck down school prayer in *Engel*, it failed to cite a single precedent.

From that point, the use of precedents by the Court has been haphazard and unpredictable. Quite simply, the Court makes its decisions almost solely on the basis of its own current prejudices rather than with any regard to original intent. In fact, when invoking authority for its decisions, it almost exclusively cites only its own recent case law.[15]

Stone v. Graham, 1980

Of course, the evil snowball from hell (Engel v. Vitale) had to pick up the Ten Commandments in its path with Stone v. Graham:

In *Stone v. Graham*, the U.S. Supreme Court on November 17, 1980, ruled (5-4) that a Kentucky statute requiring school officials to post a copy of the Ten Commandments (purchased with private contributions) on the wall in every public school classroom in the state violated the establishment clause of the First Amendment, which is commonly interpreted as a separation of church and state.[16]

Let's Not Run the Risk of a Child Learning That It's Wrong to Lie, Steal, or Murder!

Here's just one more (of thousands!) court case I would have to put in the category of *frivolous but evil:* I just coined a new word – *frevilous*!

D. DeSpain v. DeKalb County Community School District

A kindergarten teacher dared to recite the following poem with her class in 1967:

> *We thank you for the flowers so sweet;*
> *We thank you for the food we eat;*
> *We thank you for the birds that sing;*
> *We thank you for everything.*[17]

I wonder if this kindergarten teacher had inserted the words, "Big Bang," after every "thank you," it would have satisfied the parents who brought this *frevilous* lawsuit?

As a child, I recall reciting this prayer at Girl Scouts and Brownies. I learned the prayer to include *God* in the last line: *We thank you, God, for everything.* Perhaps this teacher was attempting to be politically correct by leaving out the name of God. Of course, I don't know if that was her intent, but I do know that appeasement and half – obedience never work out like we hope.

The case alleges that the teacher required the students to fold their hands in their laps and close their eyes before reciting the poem. (She really crossed the line there!)

The case further alleges that the parents do not believe in the existence of a divine being who hears or responds to prayers or supplications, and that the recitation of the daily prayer constitutes the establishment of a religious practice, thus inhibiting the free exercise of plaintiffs' religious beliefs and practices. [17]

48   DISCOVER THE HOLY SPIRIT

I've taught five-year-olds in various settings in the old days and now. I can tell you that in today's world, kids have trouble mustering the self-control to simply settle down to a meal. Placing their hands in their laps to wait until everyone is served would be a nice calm way to model self-control and empathy. Also, thankful attitudes are hard to come by in today's *it's all about me* environment. As a parent, I would be very grateful to the teacher who required a thankful, respectful, non-chaotic atmosphere at mealtime.

I have to share some anecdotal evidence of this lack of self-control and empathy among kids in the post Engel v. Vitale and post DeSpain v. Dekalb world:

I served as a camp counselor for a few summers at a camp where all the kids ate together *family style*. I can tell you that term did not compute with the kids attending the camp for the first time. The kids sat at tables of about twelve. The pots of food were placed in the middle of the table. The kids were instructed to *pass* the dishes. You would have thought they were being asked to eat standing on their heads! They had difficulty grasping the concept of serving themselves, then passing to the next person. Their inclination was to reach over whomever was in their way until they reached what they wanted. If there was a dish in front of them they didn't want, then to heck with everybody else. It didn't occur to them to pass the food in case someone else wanted it. Lack of empathy is just one of the consequences of a godless society. Thankfully, the campers quickly learned how to consider others after some good counseling. They just needed to be taught! They're trainable; but there just aren't enough parents who have been trained themselves. Yes, godly teaching affects everything, even pot- passing (and I don't mean the kind you smoke!)

I was in first grade when the fateful Engel v. Vitale ruling went down. I'm happy to say I was raised in the *Bible Belt*. We didn't feel the ruling of Engel v. Vitale until many years later. Some might say that was due to ignorance of the ruling, but knowing the administrators we had in those days, I think it was probably due to righteous indignation. Most of our school administrators were Christian in the 60's and 70's. In my public high school, in the early 70's, we still opened our school day with a scripture reading over the P.A system. When I learned of this court case as an adult, my first instinct was to be angry at my parents' generation. How could they let this happen? This is clearly a scheme of Satan to insure all future generations are ignorant of the Word of God! I later realized my anger was just a tad hypocritical since my generation had been no better. We stood by and watched our nation spiral toward hell at a pace faster than any of our ancestors could have imagined. I also remember reading about Moses following God's call to lead the Israelites out of slavery in Egypt. God parted the Red Sea, making a path (on DRY land, no less!) for the Israelites to escape Pharaoh's army. God led them with a pillar of cloud by day and a pillar of fire by night. He made undrinkable water sweet, and He sent daily bread from Heaven among many other miracles. But what did the people do when Moses was delayed coming off the mountain after receiving the Ten Commandments? They decided to adopt the pagan world view of their time. That would require removing all their gold rings from their ears in order to fashion a golden calf as their new god. This new god would take over to lead them to the Promised Land. Seems absurd doesn't it? How ungrateful! What a short memory they had! How stupid to think something they made with their hands could become their god!

I guess before we get too critical of the generation of Engel v. Vitale, or the generation of Israelites escaping slavery, we should look in the proverbial mirror of Americans in the 21st century. Our nation was founded on God's precepts. God was acknowledged in our founding documents, on our monuments, on our currency, and honored in the establishment of our government. Does anyone dare to deny the blessed status of America? Consider the beauty, the natural resources, the ability to be self-sufficient, (if only we wouldn't allow godless nations to buy our land and infiltrate us with evil-doers – but that's another book for another day!) and the most effective form of government known to mankind! The founders designed our government with godly discernment and God blessed it! Yet today our culture denies His very existence. We've removed Him from our places of learning, from our government institutions, from our homes, and from our hearts. Oh, how it must grieve the heart of God!

We all know the cliché defining insanity: If we keep doing what we've been doing, we'll keep getting what we've been getting – chaos, ignorance, death, destruction, and bondage to sin.

Let's give the Holy Spirit a chance! The results will be love, joy, peace, patience, kindness, goodness, faithfulness, gentleness, and self-control. Who doesn't want that?

Chapter 4

The Aftermath of Engel v. Vitale

We've now entered the sixth decade following this momentous decision based on misconstrued information. Having lived through the entire history since Engel v. Vitale, I have first-hand perspective.

The 60's and 70's will be remembered for racial unrest, involvement in an ill-conceived war in Viet Nam, riots in the streets, the assassination of three of our beloved leaders, the Watergate scandal, the resignation of a president, and Roe v. Wade. The 60's also ushered in the hippie movement, introducing widespread use of illicit drugs, open sexual expression, and a general confusion regarding moral and spiritual absolutes. In a nutshell, it was a time marked by indifference toward God's Word – the beginning of the downward spiral in which we still find ourselves. I contend indifference is one product of ignorance. Ignorance of God's Word breeds chaos and confusion. Chaos and confusion cause mankind to come up with its own rules for living, which only feed lusts and selfish desires. And of course, that leads to the state of depravity we're in now. The Viet Nam war was technically not a war; it was called a *conflict* because Congress never declared it a war, as mandated by the Constitution. I suspect the families of the 58,000+ names on the Viet Nam Memorial would consider it a war. But doesn't *conflict* sound better than war? Those young men who weren't killed or maimed suffered from long term effects from Agent Orange exposure, addiction to drugs and/or alcohol, psychological damage, suicide, or the antipathy their own generation showed them when they returned home. I can't think of anything positive that came out of that war. I was hoping our leaders would at least learn what *not* to do in subsequent wars but that was not to be. Afghanistan made that very clear.

In the Book of Revelation, the final book of the Bible, Jesus reveals to the Apostle John customized letters to seven churches. In the letter to the church in Laodicea, who was in a state of apostasy (desertion from the laws of God), Jesus makes it clear how He feels about indifference: *I know your deeds, that you are neither cold nor hot, I wish you were either one or the other! So, because you are lukewarm – neither hot nor cold – I am about to spit you out of my mouth* (Revelation 3:15-16). Every time I see that scripture, I think of the time when I was a little kid, early 1960's, when I was in the drug store on Main Street with my mom and my older sister. There were two water fountains in the store, a tall one that gave cool water, and a short one that said *Colored Only*. Well, my sister, (the middle child!) was determined to be a rebel, and drink from the *Colored Only* fountain. She reported that it was lukewarm and she wanted to spit it out. Lukewarm water is neither healing nor refreshing. I get it, Jesus!

In the 70's, I recall the favorite new buzz term in education – **Self Esteem.** Self confidence is a great thing. One of the fruits of the spirit is self-control. We can have a positive self image once we take hold of who we are in Christ Jesus.

Self esteem, like any other lovely-sounding term, can be afflicted with Satan's influence and twisted into something detrimental to our well-being. Here are just a few examples of the demonic twisting of righteous language.

What is right in the child's eyes is right for him or her. The idea that we are all God's children was replaced with phrases like, *You are special. There's no one else like you. You are beautiful.* Sure, those are lovely thoughts, and true, but when those words are not grounded in the Word of God, they are meaningless. Those ideas get contorted into messages such as, *Do what feels right to you. You're beautiful just the way you are* (even when you're behaving badly). *If that's YOUR truth, then it's truth. My body, my choice.* And then, those who feel conflicted in their sin often use phrases like: *Doesn't God want me to be happy?* or *God made me this way.*

The results are easy to see: The 70's generation began the decline of empathy and produced children who esteem themselves above everything and everyone, including God.

The self-esteem movement ushered in the No personal accountability era (We're still in that era!)

1999 ushered in a new phenomenon called Mass School Shootings. Our nation was in a state of shock and disbelief that this could happen in America. We were glued to our TV's, listening to the horrific events of the Columbine High School murders. We had no idea this was just the beginning of many more to come. The Washington Post reports there have been 386 school shootings since Columbine, estimating more than 356,000 students have experienced gun violence in their schools. There were more school shootings in 2022 (46) than in any year since 1999. [18] Needless to say, the problem isn't getting better.

Keep in mind, the kids who grew up in the 60's and 70's, sequestered from the Word of God, became parents of kids raised in the 80's and 90's. The kids of the 80's and 90's have had very little training in the Word because their parents were ignorant of it. Now, the kids of the 80's and 90's are raising kids in the 21st century, two generations away from the institutional stifling of God's Word. With each generation, the Word of God gets more and more watered down and misunderstood. The level of ignorance is now so obvious, it can't be ignored. We are reaping horrendous consequences as a result of removing God from our children's lives. I find it so interesting and sad that we live in the information age, where most anything we want to know is literally at our fingertips, yet we have become an increasingly ignorant people. I know some of you are saying, *Speak for yourself!* But I ask you to consider the obvious decline in critical thinking skills among our young. It's not their fault; the generations before them allowed them to be robbed of wise teaching. Along the way, we lost our way. We've now exchanged teaching children *how* to think, to teaching them *what* to think. To test my conjecture, I ask you to consider a few scenarios requiring basic critical thinking skills, and ask yourself how most **publicly** educated young adults would fare in these little tests, **without** the use of electronic devices:

1) Give oral directions to a location across town.
2) Make change for a cash transaction.
3) Devise the most efficient plan for completing a task like landscaping, warehousing, transporting product, or cleaning a house within a timeframe.
4) Organize an event within an established budget.
5) Write a thesis-driven research paper, supported with factual citations.
6) Tell an original joke without the use of foul language or insults.

Those are scenarios involving knowledge or learned skills; what about scenarios requiring wisdom? There's a big difference in those two concepts. Wisdom comes from knowing God; He is the source. Just for fun, here's an excerpt from a children's poem about the difference between wisdom and knowledge. You might want to share it with a child in your life.

Knowledge or Wisdom?

(excerpt)

Sandra F. McClure

Knowledge can come from reading a book,
Or following a recipe when you cook.
But wisdom is a very different thing;
It's knowing the right words for a friend having a bad day,
Or helping someone in just the right way.
You show knowledge when you memorize the words to a song,
But wisdom means knowing how to get along.
Knowledge allows you to quote lots of facts,
But wisdom is more about how you act.
Knowledge is knowing how many days are in a week;
Wisdom is knowing when to be quiet and when to speak.
Knowledge is knowing how to spell.
Wisdom knows when to keep a secret, and when to tell.

Back to our little test for young adults, sans electronic devices, you may be wondering why I included telling a joke. Have you noticed the slow death of comedy in our culture? God made smiles and laughter, and I am a firm believer that if God created it, there's a good reason. I don't know about you, but laughter is important to me. Laughter is a way to decompress in this intense world of unpleasantness and sadness. Without seeing that all-important hindsight humor after surviving a tough situation, we are forced to dwell in the toughness rather than overcoming the absurdity and learning from it. By the way, Proverbs 17:22 tells us *A cheerful heart is good medicine.* And Ecclesiastes 3:4 says, [There is] *a time to weep and a time to laugh.*

Over the last eight years or so, I've noticed even our highest paid comedians have lost their ability, or perhaps the will, to make us laugh. They seem to be more bent on glorifying hate and slandering those they don't like. There's nothing funny about that. Maybe it's a good time for them to Check Their Motives! Several years ago, I heard at least two major comedians share that they had decided to remove college campuses from their stand-up schedules. I contend it's because the kids don't get jokes anymore, plus it's become unsafe on college campuses to say something that might be construed to hurt fragile feelings. There's a difference between making fun of someone, and slandering someone. I guess knowing the difference requires a level of discernment missing from our 21st century culture. Bottom Line: We can no longer *take a joke*.

Empathy is another emotion I would add to the endangered list. Dictionary.com defines empathy: *the psychological identification with or vicarious experiencing of the emotions, thoughts, or attitudes of another.* Empathy manifests itself as common courtesy, putting yourself in the shoes of others, consideration of others' feelings, etc. It can also be defined by The Golden Rule.

We see empathy missing in every aspect of our lives from the inconsiderate driver to the uncaring customer service agent, to the indifferent medical professional, and every other life encounter. How do we learn empathy? Good parents modeling empathy in the home is the primary method. Children need to see their parents show empathy to them, to their family, to friends, neighbors, and other drivers on the road, etc. Also, kids don't always see empathy modeled in their classrooms, which is not surprising since the concept of empathy is missing in many young teachers' lives; they can't teach what they don't know. In my experience teaching 6th graders, I dared to mention The Golden Rule in homeroom one day. Their empty faces prompted me to mention it in every class, (I love experiments!) followed by the question, "Does anyone know what The Golden

Rule is?" Well, my little query revealed one student out of 152 knew what it meant. I'm pretty sure *every* student in my own 6th grade class (in 1968) would have known The Golden Rule.

The Golden Rule: Do unto others as you would have others do unto you. Matthew 7:12

I know I seem pretty tough on the generations behind me. I admit that is easy to do when we reach a certain level of *maturity*. I try not to be the *Stay off my lawn* stereotype, but I contend we've reached the point of absurdity in our collective moral values, and our children are suffering! But let me stop here to acknowledge that there are many young parents of the 21st century who are standing firm against the schemes of Satan and raising their children to honor God, even as the world fights against them at every turn. The problem is – there just aren't enough of them! A personal word to those parents: I know many of you, and I have tremendous respect and admiration for you! You are our true heroes! *Stay strong in the Lord and the power of His might* (Ephesians 6:10)! God bless you.

I have a unique perspective in the world of public education because 1) I'm old enough to have witnessed the systematic, intentional, demonic downfall of education in America following Engel v. Vitale (I was there at the outset), 2) I received the old school education, but I became a trained educator (in my 50's) under the new system of godless education, and 3) I've taught in the godless system in the 21st century.

During the pandemic, I think the public became more aware of the abominable state of public education in this country. Hearing the teachers' union reps doing their best to keep teachers from having to return to work was the catalyst for much outrage among parents. The only positive thing I can think of that came from the sham home-learning experience was that parents got a glimpse at the true motives of many unionized educators. Were they really thinking of the children? If only they would CHECK THEIR MOTIVES! Dedicated, hardworking educators deserve our respect and support. I'm thankful to live in a right-to-work state where educators are not beholden to union bosses. Many teachers and administrators in my home state are trying their level best to do what is right for their students, but just like God-fearing parents, their numbers are dwindling.

Here are a few examples from my personal experiences, demonstrating ignorance about God (and the victory of Satan) in the godless 21st century classroom:

In my college classes (2008-2010) that were supposed to prepare me to teach in the English Language Arts classroom, I was introduced to the new world of Young Adult novels. Being certified to teach in the middle and high school Language Arts classroom meant that I had to use the newest young adult novels in my lesson plans. I was absolutely sickened by the filthy language and the perversions that were glorified in these books. I won't list the numerous titles here because I don't want to glorify them any further.

I eventually taught 6th grade Language Arts. I was the oxymoronic teacher on the team: I was the oldest, yet the rookie. We had weekly planning meetings among the Language Arts teachers. One week, we were planning to teach a story that took place in the year 79 AD. The leader of our group made it very clear that we were not to use the term *A.D.* when teaching the story because the correct new terms for identifying time is *BCE* meaning *Before Common Era* and *ACE* meaning *After Common Era*. The textbook stated the story took place in *79 ACE*. That didn't set well with me for two reasons: 1) Those terms are just stupid, and 2) Re-writing history and the world's lexicon to please Satan and dishonor God will not be something I will teach my students. But I remained quiet. The lead teacher went on to say, *AD means After Death*. I bit my lip and left the meeting. I didn't want to embarrass him, but a language arts teacher should know that

AD doesn't mean After Death. It stands for Anno Domini, Latin for *The year of the Lord*. That was my first direct mandate to squelch any mention of God. I went back to my room and prayed (Who says we can't pray in school!) that in every class, a student would ask me what *79 ACE* meant. My prayer was answered in the affirmative; a student asked about it in every class! I fought back tears every time. It may seem like a very minor thing, but for one moment in each class, I was able to share truth to 152 students who have been victims of Satan's efforts to keep them ignorant. When the student would ask what *ACE* meant, I made it a very big point to say, "I'm SO glad you asked that question!" in an effort to cover myself in the event I was accused of initiating the discussion. I followed up by telling them that it was an effort to change the original term – A.D. And in every class, someone would boldly shout, *That means After Death!* That opened the door for me to teach them that B.C. means Before Christ and that Jesus's birth changed the very marking of time! And I told them Jesus was on earth 33 years before His crucifixion and resurrection, so if A.D. meant After Death, what happened to the accounting of those 33 years? It means The Year of the Lord! They were like little sponges soaking up this simple bit of information that had been kept from them.

Over the years since Engel v. Vitale, as the behavior became increasingly deplorable, I noticed the school systems making silly attempts to put the proverbial Band-Aid on the cancer, by implementing programs like *No Child Left Behind*. My local school district implemented Band-Aids like *Character Word of the Week*. I imagine some task force came up with that idea in hopes of changing student behavior. If we teach them definitions of character words, it's bound to improve behavior, right? Truth Alert: Teaching kids the definition of the word, honesty, will not make them honest. It's merely another piece of information. When will we stop looking for spiritual solutions with worldly ideas?

As I'm writing these pages, I'm hearing on the news some information I just have to share with you! I wish I could adequately share all the *non-coincidences* the Holy Spirit has allowed me to see and hear throughout this writing. I want everyone to experience that miraculous gift of God! The news I heard today is from the New York City mayor. He is announcing a new program to be implemented in NYC schools. Each school will dedicate two-five minutes per day to *mindful breathing*. The mayor said it will *Improve mental health and well-being.* Yep – another Band-Aid on cancer! Don't get me wrong; I am an advocate of breathing, especially mindful breathing! Seriously, I do appreciate the benefits of mindful breathing. However, I contend this is just one more desperate attempt to cure the symptoms without identifying the disease. Recent testing of thirteen-year-old students in ten NYC schools revealed the following test scores: [19]

Reading – 256/500 [51%]   Math – 271/500 [54%]

There's not enough breath in New York City to transform the illiterate to literate, or cause students to become critical thinkers, or soften their hearts to keep them from stealing, killing, and maiming anyone in their path for no apparent reason. And, ironically the five minute breathing time is to replace five minutes of literacy instruction (See Reading Scores above!). Wouldn't P.E. be a better option for the breathing exercise?

Here's an idea: Implement five minutes of Holy Bible scripture reading and prayer each day. What's to lose? Do it as an experiment. I have no doubt behavior will improve; test scores will improve; and would-be criminals will be transformed.

Here's one more horrifying and sad statistic recently reported from the city of Baltimore:

Student testing in the spring of 2023 revealed that in thirteen Baltimore City high schools, there was NOT ONE student who scored *proficient* in math. No, not one! [20]

I fear we are becoming so bombarded with news like this that we are becoming de-sensitized and hopeless. Have we given up? Maybe if we just throw more federal tax dollars into computers for every child or give teachers a pay increase, surely that will motivate kids to learn math skills, right?

If our children are headed for a cliff, is it better to build a fence at the top of the cliff, or to run an ambulance service at the bottom? [21]

Now that we've sentenced over two generations to a life ignorant of God's teaching, we see all kinds of reactive measures that do very little to change students' behavior.

Title 1 is one such costly reaction. The label of Title 1 is given to schools across the nation based on the number of students who receive free or reduced lunches. Being labeled Title 1 means federal money pours in to the school. I know of entire school districts labeled as Title 1. In his budget proposal for 2022, President Biden asked Congress to more than double the amount spent on Title I grants from $16.5 billion to $36.5 billion. [22]

So, the act of asking for free lunch triggers all kinds of funds for all kinds of reasons. I'll leave it up to you to speculate how many of the free lunch requests represent a legitimate need. I do know through observation of educational trade shows, that vendors of learning materials and other school supplies love Title 1 schools because they buy everything! I suspect if you check the junk closets of many Title 1 schools, you'll see thousands of dollars of unused learning materials that were purchased just because they could. Once the federal government opens the flood gates to pour money into their lovely-sounding programs, the vultures start circling. And our kids just keep spiraling further into the abyss of ignorance.

What have we achieved from all this funding since 1965?

Lower test scores, more drop-outs, 1619 Project, Critical Race Theory, Big Bang Theory, school massacres, TransKids ...

According to a survey conducted in the years 2011-2014, about one in five U.S. adults (21%) have *low literacy skills*, translating to about 43.0 million adults. Of the 43 million, 26.5 million were evaluated at Level 1; 8.4 million were below Level 1, while 8.2 million could not participate in the survey either because of language barriers or a cognitive or physical inability to be interviewed.[23] We can only imagine how much greater the illiteracy rate is at this writing in 2023.

In the first chapter of the Book of Romans, the Apostle Paul describes the condition of a culture who no longer sees fit to acknowledge God. See if this looks familiar?

> *The wrath of God is being revealed from Heaven against all the godlessness and wickedness of men who suppress the truth by their wickedness, ... For since the creation of the world God's invisible qualities – His eternal power and divine nature – have been clearly seen, being understood from what has been made, so that men are without excuse, For although they knew God, they neither glorified Him as God nor gave thanks to Him, but their thinking became futile and their foolish hearts were darkened. Although they claimed to be wise, they became fools Therefore God gave them over in the sinful desires of their hearts to sexual impurity for the degrading of their bodies with one another.* **They exchanged the truth of God for a lie, and worshiped and served created things rather than the Creator –** *who is forever praised. ... Furthermore, since* **they did not think it worthwhile to retain the knowledge of God, He gave them over to a depraved mind,** *to do what ought not to be done. They have become* **filled with every kind of wickedness, evil, greed and depravity.** *They are full of envy, murder, strife, deceit and malice. They are gossips, slanderers, God-haters, insolent, arrogant and boastful; they*

invent ways of doing evil; they disobey their parents; they are senseless, faithless, heartless, ruthless. Although they know God's righteous decree that those who do such things deserve death, they not only continue to do these very things but also approve of those who practice them.

Romans 1:18, 20-22, 24-25, 28-32 (NIV)

Let's break down just a few of the prophetic declarations from Romans, Chapter One (above), juxtaposed with one example from our modern-day reality:

Exchange truth for lies (v. 25) –

The truth is God created the heavens and the earth. The lie taught to our children is that the earth, with all its symbiotic complexities beyond our human comprehension, was formed by a cosmic explosion, referred to as the Big Bang. It seems the word, theory, is added to soften the lie. Nevertheless, the Big Bang *Theory* is taught as fact to our children. After searching The *Big Bang Theory*; here's a sampling of what I saw:

The universe sprang into existence some 13.7 billion years ago. While the majority of the astronomical community accepts the theory, there are some theorists who have alternative explanations besides the Big Bang – such as eternal inflation or an oscillating universe.[24]

Just for fun, I searched *Alternative explanations besides the Big Bang.* I never saw a note of any kind stating that there could possibly be a master creator, nor did I see a comment that even said, *Some people believe in a divine creator.* However, I did see a statement conflicting the age of the earth noted in my first search (13.7 billion years) with a revised age found in my second search (13.8 billion years) – a mere 100-million-year difference! [25]

THIS JUST IN! (You can't make this stuff up!) I had just written the above data regarding the scientific age of the earth as it is taught to our children. One day later, the Holy Spirit caused me to tune in to a late night TV show that quoted this new finding, below. Brace yourself, friends; as we slept, the universe doubled in age!

Our newly-devised model stretches the galaxy formation time by a several billion years, making the universe 26.7 billion years old, and not 13.7 as previously estimated, says author Rajendra Gupta, adjunct professor of physics in the Faculty of Science at the University of Ottawa. [26]

As a former language arts teacher, I can't imagine how I would teach students to obtain sources for their research papers in this environment. In a public school, would I be allowed to suggest or even accept research from a faith-based website, especially if it relates to creation? I wasn't even allowed to say *BC* and *AD*!

Worship and serve created things rather than the Creator - (v. 25)

Just a few of the created things worshipped in the 21st century are the stars (astrology), the earth, animals, crystals, the sun and the moon. And of course, there are many things individuals worship, without calling it worship, such as money, sports, people, drugs, lifestyles, climate change, science, etc.

They think it not worthwhile to retain the knowledge of God – (v. 28)

God was systematically and deliberately removed from institutions of learning and governing. Even the Ten Commandments became illegal to display. So God *gave them over to a depraved mind.*

Filled with every kind of wickedness, evil, greed, depravity, envy, murder, strife, deceit, malice – (v. 29)

Trafficking of children is the fastest growing criminal enterprise in the world, and the U.S. is one of the top three destination countries for child exploitation. In the last two years, 85,000 unaccompanied children have been allowed in our country without vetting or background checks.[27] These children are unknown and unaccounted for. It grieves me to know our government is a willing participant in sex slavery and deadly drug trafficking.

In just one American city, New York, the drug overdose deaths are reported to be 2,668 in 2021 compared to 2,103 in 2020. There were 1,370 confirmed overdose deaths in the first half of 2022. But, not to worry – The NYC Health Department is on top of it! They've launched a new vending machine program, stocked with free items any drug addict might want such as crack pipes, *safe* sex kits, toiletries, Narcan, etc. I don't think you'll be surprised to learn that the first machine was cleaned out overnight.[28] This is the explanation for this brilliant idea from the New York Health Department:

> *The Brooklyn vending machine is the latest tool to reduce stigma and barriers to services in the fight to reduce the number of overdose deaths by 2025.*[29]

Let's not fix the problem; let's just reduce the stigma. Giving free crack pipes will surely do it! I think that's what it means to be given over to a *depraved mind* (Romans 1:28).

When Satan's influence wins out over God's wisdom, chaos, confusion and a divided mind result. Here are just a few examples of the institutional schizophrenia resulting from Satan's influence on the Supreme Court:

» *It is constitutional for congressional chaplains to pray* (Marsh v. Chambers, 1983), **but unconstitutional for students to read those prayers** (State Board of Educ. v. Board of Educ. of Netcong, 1970).

» *It is constitutional to display the Ten Commandments on public property* (Anderson v. Salt Lake City Corp., 1973), **but unconstitutional either to allow students to see them** (Stone v. Graham, 1980) **or to display them at a courthouse** (Harvey v. Cobb County, 1993).

» *It is constitutional to begin public meetings with invocations* (Bogen v. Doty, 1979, and Marsh v. Chambers, 1983), **but unconstitutional to allow students to hear invocations in a public meeting** (Lee v. Weisman, 1992 and Harris v. Joint School Dist., 1994).[30]

The Information Age

Sandra F. McClure

Knowledge abounds; wisdom eludes;
A nation robbed of its soul.
Treading on ice, dazed and confused,
Our compass spins out of control.

Engel versus Vitale – 1962 – Jefferson's words misconstrued. [31]
Our own worst enemy, we welcomed him in
To rob us of truth and glorify sin.
Our sword was buried; our breastplate cracked; [32]
Now selfish deeds considered courageous acts.

Two generations have come on board
To wander in darkness – deny our Lord;
The Word was banned – now our children can't read.
Does anyone see the irony – please!

Our defenses are weakened; our foundation crumbled.
Shall we fight the battle by stifling the humble?
How did we get to this weakened state?
Our leader, our shelter was left at the gate.

The narrow gate is closed and locked;
The acceptable door opened wide. [33]
Throngs rush through; it's what we do
In search of that which we hide.

What is it we seek; does anyone know?
Or is it we just can't say?

The answer waits on the other side
To heal our nation – restore our pride.
Shall we let Him in, or is it too late?
Can these crippled hands open the gate?

Let's give it a shot; What's to lose?
Chaos? Anger? Ignorance? Abuse?
Let's join our hands; shake clear the rust
To unlock the gate; look in His eyes with trust!

Our hands will be healed; our compass restored
If we stand on truth, and seek first our Lord! [34]
Rise up, Rise up, open the gate and welcome Him in.
Rise up, Rise up, let our prodigal nation return from sin.
Rise up, Rise up, let each candle pierce the night.
Rise up, Rise up, tell the nations we've seen the light!

Chapter 5

Getting to Know the Holy Spirit

The moment you make the decision to repent (turn) from sin and accept the salvation Jesus offers, two things happen: 1) You secure your eternal home in Heaven, and 2) You become indwelt with the Holy Spirit of God. In other words, you become the temple, or dwelling place of the Holy Spirit. Eternal life for the born again is immediate and permanent. Your salvation cannot be taken from you. Jesus says in John 10:27-28: *My sheep listen to my voice; I know them, and they follow me. I give them eternal life, and they shall never perish; no one can snatch them out of my hand.* Salvation is not a gift for you to lose once you sin again. Truth Alert – You *will* sin again! But Jesus's sacrifice covers your sins before, during, and after you confess Him as Lord of your life. Hallelujah!

While the gift of eternal life is immediate and the gift of the Holy Spirit is immediate, the understanding and interaction with the Holy Spirit is something that we must intentionally develop and strengthen over the rest of our lives. For me, it took a couple of decades as a Christian before I learned to take hold and rely on the Holy Spirit full-time. As a teenager and young adult, I guess I just didn't have the hunger to delve into Bible study, and to be painfully honest, I didn't have the faith that God was truly interested in the details of my life. Not fully relying on the Holy Spirit is the greatest regret of my life. In my 20/20 hindsight, I made many knee-jerk decisions (after praying of course!), that resulted in lifelong consequences that I could have avoided if only I had totally relied on the Holy Spirit to direct my path. You see, I prayed but I didn't pray with complete trust in God, or trust in myself to recognize His voice when He spoke to me. I prayed and then blazed my own trail, thinking surely my will was God's will. And I wasn't willing to wait on His answer (It took a long time for that *patience* fruit to ripen!). Also, I think my prayers were more of a *To Do* list for God rather than a humble attempt to align my will with His. I didn't trust that being in His will was the answer to true joy. When I attended a Bible study that impressed upon me the awesomeness of approaching the Throne of Grace, the Holy Spirit called to my attention the changes needed in my self-centered prayer life. It would have served me well to memorize the following scriptures:

> *Do not be anxious about anything, but in everything, by prayer and petition, with thanksgiving, present your requests to God. And the peace of God, which transcends all understanding, will guard your hearts and your minds in Christ Jesus.*
>
> Philippians 4:6-7 (NIV)

> *When you ask, you do not receive, because you ask with wrong motives.*
>
> James 4:3 (NIV)

Jesus forgives us of our sins, past, present, and future, but He does not turn back time for us. Sometimes we're left with uncomfortable consequences from our former life, but His mercy helps us overcome that. I was saved from my sin and He was merciful. He protected me from the punishment I deserved, and allowed me to come to appreciate His love and patience with me. Now, at my advanced age, I want to spend the rest of my days encouraging others to hit the ground running following their conversion. You do that by getting into a Bible-centered church, getting entrenched in Bible study with other believers, seeking counsel of pastors and teachers, and getting involved in a God-centered social life. A Bible study specifically for new believers would be a great first step. My first group Bible study was *Experiencing God* by Henry Blackaby. I was a wife and new mother, and that was when God hit me over the head with a new understanding of the Holy Spirit. I'm sure everyone attending that study would testify of a different experience in their *Experiencing God* journey. But that's what I mean when I tell you God meets us where we are. He knows our history, our motivations, and how we process information. In the formal education world, we are taught everyone has different learning styles. Well, God knows our learning style and His Holy Spirit accommodates us.

When I was a new believer in the late 60's, it was a sweeter time when sin wasn't glorified and crimes were punished. I never heard of Christians in the U.S. being persecuted for their beliefs. Perhaps that was due to rampant lukewarm Christianity. Many, myself included, walked the aisle of a church as a child, saying they wanted to be baptized. For this little girl, raised in the Baptist Church, it was an expected rite of passage, and I felt relieved to get my fire insurance! I did it; I got saved from hell! Hallelujah! Oh how I needed a godly mentor to encourage me and teach me to rely on the Holy Spirit from that day forward. But a wonderful thing happened about a year or two after my church profession of faith. A friend and I were walking on the Main Street sidewalk when two teenage girls approached us. They were carrying Bibles, and promptly asked us the most important question of this life: If you died today, do you know where you would spend eternity? I don't remember exactly how I answered her question, but I know she directed me to some scripture and I prayed a heartfelt prayer to receive Christ. I don't remember much more about the experience. I couldn't tell you what the girls looked like or their names. I don't even remember which way they went when we parted, but I do anticipate a beautiful reunion with them when I get to Heaven. I rarely thought of that experience for almost two decades until I was in that *Experiencing God* class. During my class homework, the Holy Spirit took me back to that day at the corner of Main and Walton Streets to let me know that was the moment of my salvation, not the obligatory march down the aisle I had made with my friends.

Spiritual Gifts

There are more benefits than I can mention when it comes to accepting the gift of Jesus. There's the gift of eternal life (Can you think of a better gift?). And there's the gift of the Holy Spirit, who resides with us. We know the Holy Spirit's presence is an often-squandered gift. But there is another gift our loving heavenly Father makes available to us – the aptly named *Spiritual Gifts*. Spiritual gifts can also fall into the often-squandered category. They are given to the believer to make us useful in the kingdom of God. They help us minister to others. Getting involved in a church is the best way to learn to use our spiritual gifts. To those who say, I don't have to go to church to be saved; I can worship alone on the beach; church is for hypocrites, etc., I say to you: Your salvation is between you and God; of course you can worship at the beach or anywhere else you go; yes, there are hypocrites at any church *and* at the beach. But we can't ignore the instruction from God, telling us not to forsake the gathering of ourselves together (Hebrews 10:25). I can speak from personal experience; I've tried it both ways – spending my Sundays at the lake and spending my Sundays in fellowship with other believers, worshipping in spirit and in truth, and I can tell you when God tells us to do something, it's for our good. Just try it His way; you won't regret it. His word also says we are to encourage one another, carry one another's burdens, pray for one another, and generally love one another to the glory of God and the strengthening of the church. Jesus refers to His believers as *The Church* or *The Body of Christ*. Please notice He does not mention the numerous denominations of believers. He's interested in the hearts of mankind, not the titles we place on the signs outside the church.

When choosing a church, simply begin with prayer, asking God where He wants you to serve and grow in your walk with Him. Ask for discernment to find a fellowship that follows the Word of God without twisting it to accommodate the world. We are to be IN the world, but not OF the world (John 17:16). Ask for discernment regarding the leadership of your prospective church; are they seeking glory for themselves or glory for God? Church is not a place to sit and be entertained; it is a place where we learn, strengthen our faith, and exercise our spiritual gifts in ministries that serve others and glorify God. I don't think it's possible to realize the full joy of knowing the Lord if we are not using our spiritual gifts in service to Him. Also, I think developing and using our spiritual gifts allows us to fully realize the fruits of the spirit – Love, joy, peace, patience, kindness, goodness, faithfulness, gentleness, and self-control. Wow! Could it be that we have just unlocked the secret to happiness? I heard on the news just this morning that there is a new app to tell us how happy we are.[35] I shudder to think of all the kids who will now be taking their *happiness* temperature through an app, rather than *seeking first the kingdom of God* (Matthew 6:33) for *all* their needs, including happiness.

Spiritual gifts should not be confused with talents. Believers and unbelievers alike are blessed with talents. Talents are natural physical or mental abilities that can be developed and honed through human efforts, although they can and should be used to the glory of God. Spiritual gifts are supernaturally given by the Holy Spirit to those who have professed Jesus as their Lord. They are meant for our edification and for the strengthening of the Body of Christ. Let's investigate what God's Word says about spiritual gifts. In the following excerpt from the book of Romans, Apostle Paul explains how each believer should use his or her gifts in the body of Christ. He uses the analogy of the human body to illustrate how our diversity should be used for unity (That would be a good political slogan, wouldn't it?) For example, the eye can't function as a nose. They have very different functions, but work together to make the whole body function. Please read Romans 12:4-8 prayerfully:

> *Just as each of us has one body with many members, and these members do not all have the same function, so in Christ we who are many form one body, and each member belongs to all the others. We have different gifts, according to the grace given us. If a man's gift is prophesying let him use it in proportion to his faith. If it is serving, let him serve; if it is teaching, let him teach; if it is encouraging, let him encourage; if it is contributing to the needs of others, let him give generously; if it is leadership, let him govern diligently; if it is showing mercy, let him do it cheerfully.*

To recap, prophesying, serving, teaching, encouraging, giving, leadership, and mercy are the gifts mentioned above. What would the world be like without believers exhibiting these gifts? I wouldn't want to live in it.

Paul's epistle to the Ephesians in chapter 4:11-14 explains further:

It was he [Jesus] who gave some [gifts] to be apostles, some to be prophets, some to be evangelists, and some to be pastors and teachers, to prepare God's people for works of service, so that the body of Christ may be built up until we all reach unity in the faith and in the knowledge of the Son of God and become mature of the fullness of Christ. Then we will no longer be infants, tossed back and forth by the waves, and blown here and there by every wind of teaching and by the cunning and craftiness of men in their deceitful scheming.

Recap above gifts: apostleship, prophecy, evangelism, pastoral (shepherding), teaching, service

I don't want to be like an infant tossed to and fro by every kind of new age idea imaginable! (Pardon me here, but everything reminds me of a song: *You've got to stand for something or you'll fall for anything* (Aaron Tippin, 1990). Those words are so true! I believe God created mankind with an inherent need for a relationship with Him (After all, that's why He created us – for relationship). If we're not taught to know who God is, we'll instinctively look for something to fill that need for fatherly guidance and a sense of belonging. I ask you to just take a moment to think of all the groups available to our kids who are more than willing to provide that needed sense of belonging: drug cartels, sex traffickers, gangs, etc. – You get the idea! We are not powerless to these influencers. We just have to *Be strong in the Lord and the power of His might* (Ephesians 6:10).

IDENTIFYING YOUR SPIRITUAL GIFTS

There are some online surveys available to help identify spiritual gifts. I recently took one of these surveys. It was 80 multiple choice questions. I found it to be helpful. I hope you will too. (See Notes/Citations for an example of the survey.[39]) If you find a survey online, it should look similar to this one.

The Spiritual Gifts in My Mother

Jesus came that we may have life and have it abundantly (John 10:10). When I was a kid, I probably would have interpreted that to mean He would make sure we had abundant wealth. We were poor by worldly standards, not because my dad didn't have a decent job, but because he was an alcoholic. It's hard to believe someone could drink and smoke their entire paycheck away, but of course, we see it happen all the time. I'll never forget the look on my mother's face when she came across my dad's W-2 one day. It was a look of sheer heart-break. I knew something was wrong, but I was only eight or nine, so I simply asked, "What's that?" She said, "It's a W-2 form." I could tell she was holding back tears, so I asked no more questions. Then, when I was old enough to know what a W-2 was, I recalled that moment and wept to think of her suffering alone as she worked so hard to provide for us. Dad made a good salary, but we never knew it. My mother was indwelt with the Holy Spirit all my life. I see now how He guided her to run interference for her three girls every day, protecting us, and providing for us with a supernatural physical and spiritual strength. She would sew all night if necessary to keep all three of us in clothes, not scrappy-looking clothes, but clothes that looked store-bought. She did experience the abundant life, but it sure didn't look like it to a kid who was totally embarrassed to have friends over to see the coal-burning stove and drafty house with holes in the walls. I'm so thankful the Lord has allowed me to witness what abundant life means by God's standards.

Mother personified godly humility. She rarely made it a point to directly preach to us about God, but simply lived a life pleasing to Him. She taught by example. She let her light shine before men that they saw her good works and glorified her Father which is in Heaven (Matthew 5:16).

She was a quiet, behind-the-scenes person who never drew attention to herself. She disciplined us with gentleness. She would rarely, if ever, sit us down to have a heart-to-heart. That is the one thing I missed from her. But I try to remember that was common in her generation (The Great Depression and WWII). They just did what was right, didn't talk about it, didn't complain, and didn't get sappy about spiritual matters. Her method of discipline was to quote a scripture. Remember, His word never returns void. Here I am sixty-ish years later remembering it and sharing it. God has been so patient with me! He shows us patience and equips us (through the Holy Spirit) to be patient.

Even though Mother was always poor by worldly standards, she would say she wanted for nothing. She would say: *My God shall supply all my needs according to His glorious riches in Christ Jesus* Philippians 4:19.

Earthly riches held absolutely no importance in her life. She never asked for anything for herself. She was a giver, and a doer, and taught by example that we are not to store up treasures on earth where moth and rust destroy, and where thieves break in and steal (Matthew 6:19-21). She knew her treasure was in Heaven. She lived like her treasure was in Heaven, and she died like her treasure was in Heaven. Her spirit was fixed on eternal things, and in her last day on earth, she mustered more energy than her weak little body could have ever generated naturally. As she sang, *When the Roll is called up Yonder* in the strongest voice we had heard from her in years, knowing all the words, we knew that the same Holy Spirit that raised Jesus from the dead empowered that sweet little 100 pound body to belt out the first and second verses. Who on earth knows all the words to the second verse of that old hymn?

On that bright and cloudless morning when the dead in Christ shall rise, And the glory of His resurrection share. When His chosen ones shall gather to their home beyond the skies, And the roll is called up yonder, I'll be there. [36]

I tell you about my mom to demonstrate that God will carry us through the darkest places in this fallen world. He enables the believer to be an overcomer, and my mom is certainly an example of one. I know now that what I was witnessing was a woman filled with the Holy Spirit, able to overcome hardship, disappointment, and betrayal with grace and dignity. She exuded all the fruits of the spirit. And when she was old, her children cared for her with love and gratitude. She was so quick to say, *The Lord takes care of me*. And He certainly did! Now she's experiencing Him face to face with joy beyond our comprehension. I want to be an overcomer like my mom, where lies, betrayal, or hatred in any form cannot keep me from having the abundant life God has provided for me through Jesus. Here's my assurance that I can have that, and so can you:

These things I have spoken to you, so that in Me you may have peace. In the world you will have tribulation; but take courage, I have overcome the world.

John 16:33 (NASB)

I've heard several friends who work in the medical field tell me what an obvious difference they notice between a life with God and the life without God in their patients' last moments on earth. The life indwelt with the Holy Spirit has glorious expectations, and the one without has no hope, only fear and sadness. I've only been with two souls when they passed from this life, my mother and my sister-in-law. Both were believers. I was struck by the peaceful expression on their faces, and those expressions will never leave my memory until the day we're reunited.

What are the Roles of the Holy Spirit in our Everyday Lives?

He Prays for Us

In the last hours before His crucifixion, Jesus was thinking of us and praying to the Father on our behalf. It brings tears to my eyes as I think of Him praying for me as His brutal torture and death loomed in the hours ahead. Read John, chapter 17 for the entire prayer.

My prayer is not for them alone [the disciples]. *I pray also for those who will believe in me through their message,* [you and me] *that all of them may be one, Father, just as you are in me and I in you. May they also be in us so that the world may believe that you have sent me.*

John 17:20-21(NIV)

We are to pray without ceasing, and we are to pray, giving thanks in all circumstances (1 Thessalonians 5:17-18). And as always, He equips us to do what He instructs us to do. That's a loving Father! There have been times in my life when I didn't want to pray or couldn't pray – times when I was just so hurt or so angry, the words just didn't come. And those are the times when ...

the Spirit helps us in our weakness. We do not know what we ought to pray for, but the Spirit himself intercedes for us with groans that words cannot express. And he who searches our hearts knows the mind of the Spirit, because the spirit intercedes for the saints in accordance with God's will.

Romans 8:26-27 (NIV)

Do we serve an awesome God or what? He even helps us pray! Don't be confused when He refers to *saints*. That's you (I hope!) and me - Saints Alive! Believers who have confessed Jesus as Lord are called *saints* in the Word of God.

I have come to the place where I keep a running conversation with my Heavenly Father throughout the day. I pray about everything. You can too. Some might see these prayers as *foolishness*, but I have learned that if something is important to me, it's important to my Heavenly Father. He takes care of the big things and the little things. I think of Him as the loving, attentive father I longed to have as a child and young adult. Here are some random examples of prayers I might pray any day:

» Lord, go before me to this doctor's appointment. Give me the right questions to ask. Give the doctor, and every other hand that touches my case, the anointing to do the right thing according to your will.

» Let the words of my mouth and the meditation of my heart be pleasing to you.

» Help me make this left turn.

» Prepare me to teach your children in a way that pleases you. Give them a passion for learning your word and applying it to their lives.

» Lord, help me forgive those who seek to harm me. You know I can't do it in my own strength; I need your help to see them as you see them. I don't want to hold grudges; I know it only hurts me and my testimony. Thank you for your mercy on me. May I show it to others.

» Lord, help my friend who is going through crisis. Help her to take hold of the peace that transcends her understanding. Heal her mind, body and spirit. You tell us to carry each other's burdens. Show me how I can minister to her in your name.

» This is the day the Lord has made. I will rejoice and be glad in it. Thank you for your love and faithfulness throughout my life. Thank you for your mercy, new every morning.

» Lord, please keep me safe from harm and keep me from causing harm to anyone else.

» Go before me to this meeting. Help me get there on time. Work through all the circumstances and help us to make the right decisions according to your will.

» Guide my steps; guard my tongue, and help me to trust you with all my heart and lean not on my own understanding.

Just remember, He knows us better than we know ourselves. We can't surprise Him with our prayers. And of course, it's a futile act to lie to Him. He doesn't need us to pray in order to understand our situation. We need to pray to better understand Him, and to better understand our circumstances. It's amazing the things He will reveal to us in our heartfelt prayers. He doesn't always tell me what my sinful mind wants to hear, but I have come to trust it is ALWAYS for my good. He knows our needs before we ask, but it's our act of faith that unlocks His will in our lives. Jesus explains His intimate love and care for us in Luke 12:6-7:

Are not five sparrows sold for two pennies?
Yet not one of them is forgotten by God.
Indeed, the very hairs of your head are all numbered.
Don't be afraid; you are worth more than many sparrows.

If He knows every hair on our heads, we can trust Him to know our needs better than we do.

He Reveals Truth to Us

Preparing His disciples for His physical departure from them, Jesus assured them He would not leave them as orphans. He promised the Spirit of Truth as their Counselor. And yes, that applies to us too.

In the Gospel of John, Jesus tells His disciples to prepare to receive the Spirit of Truth (aka The Holy Spirit):

> *If you love me, you will obey what I command.*
> *And I will ask the Father, and he will give you another*
> *Counselor to be with you forever – the Spirit of Truth. The world*
> *cannot accept him, because it neither sees him nor knows him.*
> *But you know him, for he lives with you and will be in you.*
> *I will not leave you as orphans; I will come to you.*
>
> John 14:15-18 (NIV)

> *I have much more to say to you, more than you can now bear.*
> *But when he, the Spirit of Truth, comes,*
> *he will guide you into all truth.*
>
> John 16:12-13 (NIV)

When we can't even trust most of our news outlets to tell us the truth, it's wonderful to know the Holy Spirit will help us discern truth from lies if we just trust Him, without first allowing ourselves to be duped by the spiritual forces of evil. We can make that a matter of prayer, can't we?

My Prayer: Lord, help me discern truth in every situation. May I always be a seeker of truth before I speak or act in a harmful way. I pray my grandchildren will be seekers of truth, and learn to trust their heavenly Counselor in all circumstances.

He Convicts Us of Sin

I know the word, *convict*, doesn't have a pleasant connotation. But it's just another way He reveals truth to us. He makes it clear to us when we sin. While the believer is not immune from sin in this fallen world, we have a very effective antidote to combat it. The believer will not feel good about sinning, and the believer is compelled (by the Spirit) to confess it and make it right according to God's will. Simply put, He gives us discernment regarding right and wrong. Let's be reminded of the aforementioned scripture, Romans 8:27: *He searches our hearts...* He helps us check our motives.

He Guides Us

There is so much to say here. But I find it a difficult task to properly convey how God works through the details of the believer's life. It's such a personal thing, and so often I just don't talk about how He works out situations in my life, not because I'm not elated, but often it just boils down to a *You had to be there* story. And of course, that is what I mean when I say, *He meets us where we are.* When I think of how the creator of the universe made a way to commune with me and be a *father* to me every minute of my life, I'm just overwhelmed! We talk to kids so often about making good choices. That's one of the roles of the Holy Spirit in our lives – guiding us to make good choices. The Apostle Paul teaches us (via the Holy Spirit) to *Be careful how you walk not as unwise men but as wise, making the most of your time, because the days are evil. So then do not be foolish, but understand what the will of the Lord is* Ephesians 5:15-17 (NASB).

I am the youngest of three girls. The following story is a completely true account of events involving my two sisters and my mother. I wasn't there, but I feel like I was. I share it through the first person writing of my sister. It took place Christmas, 1983. This is just one real-life example of how God guides us and equips us for ministry, and how *He works all things together for good for those who love Him, who have been called according to his purpose* Romans 8:28.

One Account of His Guidance

It was a record-cold Christmas Eve in Georgia, and I was at work until late in the evening. The last to leave the building, I was eager to get away from the office after coordinating a catered dinner party for all the employees. I was single at the time, and headed to my mother's house for Christmas. Both my sisters were out of town, so it was a quiet Christmas – just Mother and me. On Christmas evening, we had a family emergency, compelling Mother and I to travel to the North Carolina mountains to retrieve my sister who was visiting friends in Cherokee, NC. [Keep in mind; this was before cell phones, GPS, MapQuest, etc.] So, following a long distance phone call to arrange a meeting place, we bundled up and off we went. It was getting dark, and North Georgia was experiencing snow. The weather was getting more treacherous with every mile. Warnings to stay off the roads were on the radio every minute, and power was out all over North Georgia. The increasing snow and heavy winds made for very poor driving conditions. We were on a back road in the middle of nowhere it seemed, when we heard the dreadful sound and felt the bumping of a flat tire. It happened just before a stop sign. Straight ahead of the sign was a private driveway to a country home where we chose to creep to a halt. My main concern was my elderly mother, and making sure she was warm.

I went to the front door in total darkness. A very nice lady came to the door and I explained our plight. I asked if Mother could come inside their home where it was warm while I changed the flat tire. Without hesitation, the lady said, "Sure, we don't have power, but we have a warm fire." Leaving Mother by the fire, I returned to the car and started removing the jack and the spare. Almost immediately, the Dad and his son joined me with flashlights and willing hands to help change the tire in that pitch dark, bitter cold driveway. When we had finished the task at hand, the lady told my mom, *Tell your **boy** to come in and get warm by the fire.* (That part has absolutely no relevance to the story, but as the little sister, it makes me laugh – and this story needs some comic relief! My lovely sister was identified as a boy before it was cool to identify as a boy, but with her hat pulled down over her ears and the dim lighting, I guess it was understandable. After all, that was no time for vanity!) I went in to properly thank them all for their generosity and hospitality. As we chatted, I learned they had delayed their Christmas celebration because their family couldn't get in due to the snow, but they were all expected the next day. They laughingly said, *We can't cook; our pipes are frozen and we don't know what we are going to feed everyone.* I excused myself and went back out to the car, where I retrieved a fully cooked whole turkey, a large pan of fully cooked delicious dressing, gravy, and all the side dishes a big southern family could want. The caterer at my office party had boxed up a complete untouched Christmas dinner that my boss insisted I take home. I felt guilty taking that dinner home, having no idea how it would be used, but I knew it would definitely be protected in my cold trunk. The family was ecstatic to see that beautiful Christmas dinner, shouting, *We prayed for the Lord to help us, and He sent you!*

Mother and I went on our way, safely rendezvoused with my sister, and returned home. Our family emergency worked out fine (according to God's will). But that's not the end of the story; I took my tire to the service station the next business day to have it repaired. The mechanic said, *We have looked and looked at this tire and can't find any reason it went flat; there is no hole.* With that, he re-mounted the original tire and I drove on it for thousands of miles.

God worked so many things together for good that Christmas to meet the needs of His people! That's just a sampling of how

He works. We just need to make ourselves available. He uses His people to minister to one another. That is such a beautiful truth that I want my unbelieving friends to experience.

Chapter 6

The Omnipresence of the Holy Spirit

First of all, let's understand that the Holy Spirit has always been part of God, not make-believe, not an after-thought, and not an *IT*. The Holy Spirit is a *HE* (No confusing pronouns with God!) He is one third of the holy trinity – Father, Son, and Holy Spirit. He was part of God at the creation of the world, part of God throughout the Old Testament, and part of God through the New Testament until now, and to *Infinity and Beyond!*

THE HOLY SPIRIT AT CREATION

Genesis 1:2 – *The earth was formless and void, and darkness was over the surface of the deep, and the **Spirit of God** was moving over the surface of the waters.*

Genesis 1:26 – *Then God said, Let **us** make man in **our** image, according to **our** likeness ...*

John 17:5 – (Fast forward thousands of years as Jesus prays an intercessory prayer for us in the last hours before His crucifixion) *And now, Father, glorify me in your presence with the glory I had with you before the world began.* (Jesus, the Spirit, and the Father were ONE from the beginning.)

My Prayer: Father, please help the unbeliever grasp what it means to be made in your image, with spirit in order to commune with You, with ability to reason, with the capacity to love, to work, to have compassion, to laugh, and to exercise wisdom. Thank you, Father for your presence with me. May your Word sear the hearts of unbelievers that they would come to know you.

The Holy Spirit in the Old Testament

Throughout the Old Testament, and through Jesus's ministry, the Spirit of God would come to a person at a specific time in order to accomplish a particular task or ministry. Then He would depart. The 39 books in the Old Testament were written by God's appointed prophets, historians, leaders, or poets, who were overcome by the Spirit of God in order to document God's revelations to us. Their words are God's Word. I love the beginning (Chapter 1) of the Book written by the prophet Jeremiah. He testifies of his calling to be a prophet of God:

Now the word of the Lord came to me saying, Before I formed you in the womb I knew you, and before you were born, I set you apart;
[Who says life doesn't exist in the womb?]
I appointed you as a prophet to the nations.
Ah Sovereign Lord, I said, I do not know how to speak,
I am only a child. But the Lord said to me, Do not say,
I am only a child. You must go to everyone I send you to and
Say whatever I command you ...I have put My words in your mouth.

Jeremiah 1:4-7, 9 (NIV)

Then in chapter 31 of Jeremiah, God reveals His New Covenant to be realized about six hundred years later, following the resurrection of the long-awaited Messiah Jesus. In verse 33-34, He reveals that in the future, His law will be in the hearts of mankind. In other words, the Holy Spirit will come to reside in us.

But this is the new covenant I will make with the people of Israel after those days, says the LORD. I will put my instructions deep within them, and I will write them on their hearts. I will be their God, and they will be my people. And they will not need to teach their neighbors, nor will they need to teach their relatives, saying, 'You should know the LORD.' For everyone, from the least to the greatest, will know me already, says the LORD. And I will forgive their wickedness; I will never again remember their sins.

THE HOLY SPIRIT IN THE NEW TESTAMENT AND NOW

My Prayer: There's just so much to say about your presence with us through your Holy Spirit that no book could hold it. Please help me deliver your message your way, without any self-serving interference. I need your help to keep me focused on nothing but the truth. You even help us pray when we don't know how. Thank you, Lord!

Before we discuss the giving of the Holy Spirit as a 24/7 presence with us, let's look at a general timeline:

» Jesus was crucified on Friday during Passover (AD 33)
» On the following Sunday morning, the Spirit of God raised Jesus from the dead. Jesus then appeared to His disciples and others on that day. He continued appearing to them for forty subsequent days, continuing to teach them in preparation for their ministries.

» On His final day on earth, (forty days after His resurrection from the dead) Jesus gave parting instructions to His disciples, known as *The Great Commission* (Matthew 28:18-20):

> *All authority in heaven and on earth has been given to me. Therefore go and make disciples of all nations, baptizing them in the name of the Father and of the Son and of the Holy Spirit, and teaching them to obey everything I have commanded you. And surely I am with you always, to the very end of the age.*

Further parting instructions to the disciples are reported in the book of Acts 1: 4-5, 8-9:

> *Do not leave Jerusalem, but wait for the gift my Father promised, which you have heard me speak about. For John [the Baptist] baptized with water, but in a few days you will be baptized with the Holy Spirit. ... you will receive power when the Holy Spirit comes on you; and you will be my witnesses in Jerusalem, and in all Judea and Samaria and to the ends of the earth. After he said this, he was taken up before their very eyes, and a cloud hid him from their sight.*

The Promise of the Indwelling is Fulfilled at Pentecost

About ten days after Jesus ascended into Heaven (about fifty days after His resurrection) was the day of Pentecost. *Pentecost* means *fiftieth* and refers to the feast of harvest, celebrated fifty days after Passover in May/June. At Pentecost, an offering of first fruits would be made.[40]

The disciples were gathered in a house together on the day of Pentecost. Remember, Jesus had instructed them to wait in Jerusalem until the Holy Spirit came upon them. They would not be equipped to minister in Jesus's name without that indwelling. (The same is true for us.)

Suddenly a sound like the blowing of a violent wind came from heaven and filled the whole house where they were sitting. They saw what seemed to be tongues of fire that separated and came to rest on each of them. All of them were filled with the Holy Spirit and began to speak in other tongues as the Spirit enabled them.

Acts 2:2-4 (NIV)

What a scene that must have been! Can you imagine tongues of fire resting upon each believer? And can't you imagine the selfies we would be taking if this happened to us? Look at us! Look at us!

Devout worshippers from every nation had made the pilgrimage to Jerusalem for the observance of Pentecost, never knowing the world-changing event God had brought them together to experience. The noise like a violent rushing wind drew them to gather in one place. I wonder if it was like the sound of a freight train; that's always the description we hear for an approaching tornado. The bottom line is – they experienced something only God could do. There could be no question about it. Acts 2:5-8 paints the picture for us:

Now there were staying in Jerusalem God-fearing Jews from every nation under heaven. When they heard this sound a crowd came together in bewilderment, because each one heard them speaking in his own language. Utterly amazed, they asked: Are not all these men who are speaking Galileans? Then how is it that each of us hears them in his own native language?

The subsequent scriptures in Acts 2 list at least fifteen different languages represented in the crowd. I'm imagining the United Nations gathering for a summit without the need for interpreters - everyone in the audience hearing the speaker in his or her native language. There could be no question the Spirit of God had been delivered to all who would receive Him!

Peter, who was an intimate eye witness to Jesus's crucifixion, resurrection, forty-day post-resurrection presence, and ultimate ascension to heaven, stood to deliver a powerful spirit-filled sermon to explain what Jesus had done for them, and how it fulfilled Old Testament prophecy.

When the people heard this, they were cut to the heart and said to Peter, and the other apostles, 'Brothers, what shall we do?' Peter replied, 'Repent and be baptized, every one of you, in the name of Jesus Christ for the forgiveness of your sins. And you will receive the gift of the Holy Spirit. The promise is for you and your children and for all who are far off – for all whom the Lord our God will call.' With many other words he warned them; and he pleaded with them, 'Save yourself from this corrupt generation.' [Hear this people of the 21st century!] *Those who accepted his message were baptized, and about three thousand were added to their number that day.*

Acts 2:37-41 (NIV)

And that was the beginning of the Church. The disciples were now equipped to do what Jesus had been preparing them to do for the past three years. Those of us old enough to remember the Billy Graham Crusades can imagine this crowd so vividly. Thousands responding to the leading of the Holy Spirit is a beautiful sight! Further verses in Acts, chapter 2 tell us that the new believers devoted themselves to the apostles' teaching, to fellowship, and to prayer. They continued to meet daily in the temple courts. They ate together in their homes, praising God and enjoying the company of fellow believers. And the Lord added to their numbers daily.

He promised he would never leave us. His final words before ascending to Heaven assure us He is with us always, to the very end of the age. He sent the Spirit to fulfill that promise – our personal Savior and Heavenly Father with us every minute of every day. And let's not forget the bonus of eternal life! Can I get an Amen?

Chapter 7

Sinning Against the Spirit

We can be our own worst enemy when it comes to sinning against the Spirit, or perhaps a better way to put it is – cutting off our noses to spite our faces. I love that old adage because it visually drives the point home; it's never for our good to sin against the Holy Spirit.

There are three terms the Bible uses to explain sinning against the Spirit: Quenching, Grieving, and Blaspheming the Spirit of God. I've added another category in our relationship with the Spirit of God; it's the act of questioning the Spirit. I engage in questioning quite often. He understands I can be slow to get the message sometimes, and I'm thankful for His patience!

BLASPHEMING AGAINST THE SPIRIT

Let's get the most unpleasant category out of the way first. The one who never receives/accepts Jesus does not receive the Holy Spirit. For lack of a better term, they're a package deal. Quenching and grieving the Holy Spirit are sins of the believer. We know the believer will be forgiven, and we know the believer is capable of re-kindling the Spirit in his or her life. However, Jesus makes it clear in His response to the religious teachers of the day that there is one sin that will not be forgiven – blasphemy. These teachers had accused Him of being possessed by Satan. That blasphemous accusation warranted this stern warning from the Son of God: *But whoever blasphemes against the Holy Spirit will never be forgiven; he is guilty of an eternal sin* (Mark 3:29). Denying Jesus's deity is denying the Holy Spirit.

QUENCHING THE SPIRIT

Apostle Peter gives a litany of instructions to the believer in 1 Thessalonians, 5:12-22. Among them is the admonition to NOT quench the Spirit. The NIV (New International Version) translation says, *Do not put out the Spirit's fire* (v. 19). Again, my passion for language arts gives me such an appreciation for the figurative language the Spirit uses to help us understand (I wish we were allowed to expose our students to it!). I'm also a visual learner, so as I read anything, I'm seeing an imaginary picture. I'm imagining those first believers in Acts with those *tongues of fire* over their heads, indicating the presence of the Spirit. And in my cartoonish brain, I'm imagining one of them sinning against the Spirit as his fire dwindles to a smoldering ember.

Fire is associated with energy and life. It purifies, refines, and provides warmth. It represents strength and power. Pouring water on (quenching) that power in our lives results in a painful self-inflicted wound. But He is merciful; nothing can put out the fire beyond re-kindling, because we are sealed for eternity with Him. [He] *set His seal of ownership on us, and put His Spirit in our hearts as a deposit, guaranteeing what is to come* (2 Corinthians 1:22).

How do we quench the Spirit's fire in our lives? We can do that by ignoring His leading, by repeatedly going OUR way when He is telling us to go HIS way, or by intentionally saying *No* to His leading. Let's not forget, God gave us free will. We don't give up our free will when we receive Jesus. However, when we decide to accept Jesus, which is the key to receiving His presence with us, we are confessing that we trust His will to be superior to ours. With experience, we will learn to accept and trust His leading from the outset. Saying *No* to the Holy Spirit costs us time, causes regret, and can sometimes cause irreparable damage. But it warrants repeating - His mercy is everlasting; quenching the Holy Spirit doesn't cause us to lose our salvation, and it doesn't prevent us from rekindling the Spirit. Jesus says: *My sheep listen to My voice; I know them and they follow Me* (John 10:27).

Questioning the Spirit

Note to new believers: It's normal to question your spiritual hearing, especially if you have limited knowledge of the scriptures. Don't be afraid to ask the Lord to give you discernment to know if you're hearing Him properly. Let God's Word (The Holy Bible) be your spiritual hearing aid. Tell Him you want to be attentive to His leading. He will honor that and help you tune your spiritual ears to His voice. There are a couple of facts you can rely on when questioning your spiritual hearing: 1) The Spirit will never lead you to do something that contradicts His Word, and 2) He will bring His Word to your mind at the right time. Yes, it's a trust issue. I have learned that if I'm not sure what the Lord is telling me to do, it's quite alright to wait. Don't be afraid to say, *I'll have to pray about that and get back with you.* Waiting is where we strengthen our faith muscles. Knee-jerk reactions can cause a sprain that takes you out of the game for longer than you will want. Take it from me; save the knees for prayer. You'll be glad you did. Today's world expects us to make snap decisions, but that gets us in trouble. Waiting on the Lord reaps rewards, noted in Isaiah 40:30-31:

*Though youths grow weary and tired, and vigorous young men stumble
badly, yet those who wait for the Lord will gain new strength;
they will mount up with wings like eagles,
They will run and not get tired,
They will walk and not become weary.*

There was a time in the Old Testament when a judge of Israel, named Gideon, questioned his spiritual hearing. He desperately wanted clarification of God's instruction. I think it's important to know that Gideon was not a brave person. He was rather timid and insecure in his leadership of Israel – not the best traits for the leader of a nation. But God knew what man couldn't see; Gideon had great potential. I believe that insecurity in his ability to hear God's voice is understandable – he was raised by a father who engaged in idol worship, so he would not have been raised in the knowledge of the one true God. He may have been confused as anyone would be who had been raised to believe in various false gods. We see that very clearly today, don't we? Those not raised to know and respect the Word of God think it's *foolishness* to make Him Lord of their lives. Simple Truth - Children believe what they see and hear from their parents.

Israel, circa 1043 BC, had been doing what was evil in the sight of the Lord. *Everyone did what was right in his own eyes* (Judges 17:6). Sound familiar? So, the Lord gave them over to the hands of Midian for seven years (Warning: God *does* judge nations). Gideon was faced with an enormous task – to deliver Israel from the oppression of the Midianites, who invaded their farms, ravaged their land, killed their livestock, and left them impoverished.

In his fear of drawing attention from the Midianites, Gideon was threshing his wheat in the safer shelter of the winepress rather than taking it to the large open-air threshing floor. It was there that he was approached by an angel of the Lord, who greeted him with an unusual greeting: *The Lord is with you, mighty warrior (v.12).*

I love how God addressed Gideon with the title he would later deserve following his obedience to the Lord; *mighty warrior* was certainly not the title he currently demonstrated. God then told him: *Go in the strength you have and save Israel out of Midian's hand. Am I not sending you? (v.14)* But Gideon showed insecurity in his response: *How can I save Israel? My clan is the weakest in Manasseh, and I am the least in my family (v.15).*

Each task the Lord gave Gideon to do, he was obedient, but fulfilled the task with timidity and trepidation. He seemed to have a degree of faith, but it was not very high on the faith meter. That leads us to the test that Gideon proposed to God – the fleece test. Judges 6:36-40 (NASB)–

Then Gideon said to God, If you will deliver Israel through me, as you have spoken, behold, I will put a fleece of wool on the threshing floor. If there is dew on the fleece only, and it is dry on all the ground, then I will know that you will deliver Israel through me, as you have spoken. And it was so. When he arose early the next morning and squeezed the fleece, he drained the dew from the fleece, a bowl full of water. Then Gideon said to God, Do not let your anger burn against me that I may speak once more; please let me make a test once more with the fleece, let it now be dry only on the fleece, and let there be dew on all the ground.

God did so that night; for it was dry only on the fleece and dew was on all the ground.

In my past readings of Gideon and the fleece, I marveled that God responded favorably to being tested this way, especially two times. But the Spirit drew me to this story for a fresh reading for a new reason. With fresh eyes, I have new empathy for Gideon. I suspect most believers have been in his place, wondering if we're hearing properly. We have thoughts like these: *Am I just hearing what*

I want to hear? Did He really want me to do that? I don't want to do that! I don't think I can do that. What would people think? And the questioning can go on and on. Sometimes when we hear something we don't want to do, we can suppress the thoughts, hoping the situation will go away. It can result in the aforementioned quenching of the Spirit.

But Gideon seemed to question God in a genuine effort to understand what He wanted him to do. And we must remember that God's mercy is everlasting. He is patient with us, and He honors our attempts at obedience. It seems Gideon was a novice at communing with the real God. He also knew he lacked the skills and the confidence to accomplish the enormous task he'd been given, so he wanted to be sure beyond any doubt he was hearing his assignment correctly. Leading up to the battle with the Midianites, God gave Gideon another mission that would test his mettle and prepare him for bigger assignments. He was given the task of destroying his father's altar, built to worship idols: One idol was the false deity known as Baal, usually depicted as a bull or ram, [37] and the other idol was the false goddess, Asherah, fashioned from a carved wooden pole, standing beside Baal.[38]

> *Take your father's bull and a second bull seven years old,*
> *And pull down the altar of Baal which belongs to your father,*
> *and cut down the Asherah that is beside it; and build an altar*
> *to the Lord your God on the top of this stronghold in an orderly*
> *manner, and take a second bull and offer a burnt offering with*
> *the wood of the Asherah which you shall cut down. Then Gideon*
> *took ten men of his servants and did as the Lord had spoken to him;*
> *and because he was too afraid of his father's household and*
> *the men of the city to do it by day, he did it by night.*
>
> Judges 6:25-27 (NASB)

He did it! But he did it with fear and cowardice. Thank you, Lord, for dealing with us as You see us, not as we see ourselves! It's also important to note that God gave Gideon victory over the vast number of Midianites and Amalekites (*as numerous as locusts! With camels as numerous as the sand on the seashore*! (Judges 7:12). Gideon started with 32,000 volunteers, but God said to Gideon, *The people who are with you are too many for Me to give Midian into their hands, for Israel would become boastful, saying, My own power has delivered me* (Judges 7:2). God wanted Israel to know their victory could only be attributed to God. So, through some unusual tests, the Lord culled Gideon's army to a mere three hundred soldiers! This account of Gideon brings us back to the same fact once again; God meets us where we are, even in our weakness. And He speaks to each believer in a different way according to his or her maturity and knowledge. And He equips us to do what He instructs us to do. The tests God instructed Gideon to perform in order to cull his army can seem very strange to those of us looking on thousands of years later, but I hope you will give Gideon a close reading in the book of Judges, chapters 6-8.

It is not our job to question how God operates in the lives of others. He knows our needs and He knows what is in store for our future, and we don't. So let's trust Him in His dealings with us. I'm also learning to stop second-guessing God's answer to prayer. If I earnestly pray for His will to be done in a situation, and it doesn't turn out exactly like I imagined, second-guessing the outcome could be a sign that I didn't trust Him in the first place.

Grieving the Spirit

Do not let any unwholesome talk come out of your mouths, but only what is helpful for building others up according to their needs, that it may benefit those who listen. And do not grieve the Holy Spirit of God, with whom you were sealed for the day of redemption.

Get rid of all bitterness, rage and anger, brawling and slander, along with every form of malice. Be kind and compassionate to one another, forgiving each other, just as in Christ God forgave you.

Ephesians 4:29-32 (NIV)

The above scripture follows many admonitions given to the body of Christ concerning how to treat one another. I have come to believe that nothing grieves God like seeing His children mistreat one another. As a parent, doesn't that grieve you to see your children treat each other with unforgiving spirits, bitterness, rage, anger, brawling, slander, lies, etc.? Our Heavenly Father grieves over that, too.

Please allow me to give a little heartfelt advice to those who may have grieved the Spirit and missed out on that *peace that transcends our understanding*. If grieving His Spirit has caused you to have broken relationships, please don't wait another minute to stop and pray. Tell the Lord you want to re-kindle His Spirit in your life. Ask Him to bring to your mind the things you may have done to cause the brokenness, even things you may have buried in your mind because you just didn't want to face them. Confess those sins to your loving Heavenly Father. Repent from them; that means turn and go the opposite way. Perhaps that means turning back to the person(s) you have hurt, or the person who has hurt you. Ask God to help you forgive. And ask Him to intervene to help them forgive you too. Admit to God that you can't do it on your own. Because we are sinners from birth, we have the innate ability to hold onto grudges like a warm winter coat. But as you may have learned, that coat gets heavy and hot and stinky! Throw it away! Attempt reconciliation as the Lord leads. He will give you the words. They will not be hateful, blaming, or arrogant words. They will be words of humility and love. But be prepared; even though you may be faithful, the other party may not be ready to reciprocate. If they won't take your calls, reach out in the way the Lord leads. Then pray, forgive, and wait. God will work it out in His perfect timing. He will honor your obedience and give you that peace you've been missing, the peace that transcends your understanding. If the other party refuses to reconcile, that's their burden to bear, and their lost blessing due to grieving the Spirit in their own lives. Just pray without ceasing, and trust that in His timing, peace will prevail. After all, He is the *Prince of Peace* (Isaiah 9:6).

There is an old gospel song that speaks so aptly to the consequence of unresolved sin in our lives:

Sin will take you farther than you want to go,
slowly but wholly taking control.
Sin will leave you longer than you want to stay.
Sin will cost you far more than you want to pay.[41]

Epilogue/ Final Thoughts

Thank you for taking this journey with me. My prayer is that those who thought the things of the Spirit to be foolishness have now come to realize that the real foolishness is in rejecting Jesus, thus rejecting the Spirit of God.

Without receiving Christ, we cannot receive the Holy Spirit. Without receiving the Holy Spirit, we are left to our own limited human reasoning, and we know human reasoning is intrinsically flawed by sin.

We can clearly see that our world is being overwhelmed by the evil wiles of Satan, but believers are not powerless against it. If we stand firm and put on the full armor of God, we have everything we need to overcome this unholy world.

I urge you to hit the ground running in your efforts to get to know the Lord. You do this by getting into Bible Study and joining a fellowship of mature believers who can help you in your spiritual growth.

Begin a practice of worship. John 4:24 tells us: *God is spirit, and those who worship Him must worship in spirit and truth.* Worship is a time for our spirit to commune with the Spirit of God. That means authentic worship - worship that sets aside any worldly desires to be seen, or to gain approval of men, but to reverently approach the throne of grace with heartfelt praise and gratitude. Worship can take place in many forms. That's between you and God.

Discover your spiritual gifts and use them to serve others and glorify God.

Take responsibility for raising and educating your children under the instruction of the Lord. *Train a child in the way he should go, and when he is old he will not turn from it* (Proverbs 22:6). If you don't have children of your own, ask the Lord to show you how to serve children through your spiritual gifts. As a society, we're failing them miserably, and they need our help!

Honor our nation's godly heritage. We have reaped the rewards of our forefathers' faithfulness. Let's be grateful and follow the instructions of Hebrews 13:7-8: *Remember your leaders, who spoke the word of God to you. Consider the outcome of their way of life and imitate their faith. Jesus Christ is the same yesterday and today and forever.* Those who attempt to re-invent God in order to satisfy their worldly desires do so at their peril!

After research and prayer, exercise your right to vote. Choose leaders who honor the Word of God and support godly principles. Responsible voting for local leaders is as important as our responsibility at the federal level.

I'll leave you with one final message from the words of Jesus, in His response to a question posed by the Pharisees (religious rulers):

Of all the commandments, which is the most important?
[Jesus responded] *Love the Lord your God with all your heart and with all your soul and with all your mind and with all your strength. The second is this: Love your neighbor as yourself. There is no commandment greater than these.*

Mark 12:28b, 30-31 (NIV)

Notes/Citations

1 https://www.cdc.gov/suicide/suicide-data-statistics.html

2 "Pierre Teilhard de Chardin Quotes." BrainyQuote.com. BrainyMedia Inc, 2023. 22 April 2023. https://www.brainyquote.com/quotes/pierre_teilhard_de_chardi_160888

3 https://www.goodreads.com/quotes/329896

4 MacArthur, John. 2006. *The MacArthur Study Bible*. Thomas Nelson, Inc., p.1784.

5 https://www.guinnessworldrecords.com/world-records/best-selling-book-of-non-fiction

6 https://www.statista.com/statistics/185274/number-of-legal-abortions-in-the-us-since-2000/

7 https://www.historyonthenet.com/what-were-the-josef-mengele-experiments

8 https://www.youtube.com/watch?v=S9NoQHgjM_0&t=19s

9 Wallbuilders.com. 2008.

10 Barton, David. *Original Intent: The Courts, the Constitution, & Religion*. (Aledo, TX: Wallbuilder Press, 2008), 168.

11 Barton, David. *Original Intent: The Courts, the Constitution, & Religion*. (Aledo, TX: Wallbuilder Press, 2008), 51-52.

12 Barton, David. *Original Intent: The Courts, the Constitution, & Religion*. (Aledo, TX: Wallbuilder Press, 2008), 161.

13 https://study.com/academy/lesson/engel-v-vitale-in-1962-summary-facts-decision.html

14 Barton, David. *Original Intent: The Courts, the Constitution, & Religion*. (Aledo, TX: Wallbuilder Press, 2008), 162.

15 Barton, David. *Original Intent: The Courts, the Constitution, & Religion*. (Aledo, TX: Wallbuilder Press, 2008), 197.

16 https://www.britannica.com/event/Stone-v-Graham

17 https://law.justia.com/cases/federal/district-courts/FSupp/255/655/1818129/

18 https://www.washingtonpost.com/education/interactive/school-shootings-database/

19 https://www.foxnews.com/video/6330290171112

20 https://foxbaltimore.com/amp/news/project-baltimore/at-13-baltimore-city-high-schools-zero-students-tested-proficient-on-2023-state-math-exam

21 Steve Whipple, Pastor to Students, 2005

22 https://thehill.com/policy/finance/553405-biden-goes-big-on-title-i-funding-for-low-income-students/

23 https://nces.ed.gov/pubs2019/2019179/index.asp

24 https://www.space.com/25126-big-bang-theory.html

25 https://www.space.com/24781-big-bang-theory-alternatives-infographic.html

26 https://phys.org/news/2023-07-age-universe-billion-years-previously.html

27 https://www.foxnews.com/video/6330928406112

28 https://www.foxnews.com/us/new-york-city-vending-machine-offering-free-crack-pipes-drug-users-runs-out-overnight-report

29 https://www.nyc.gov/site/doh/about/press/pr2023/health-department-launches-first-public-health-vending-machine.page

30 Barton, David. *Original Intent: The Courts, the Constitution, & Religion* (Aledo, TX: Wallbuilder Press, 2008), 239.

Notes/Citations (continued)

The Information Age
By Sandra McClure

31 Engel vs. Vitale is the 1962 Supreme Court decision, declaring it unconstitutional to conduct public school-sanctioned prayers. The basis for the decision was a private letter from Thomas Jefferson to the Danbury, Connecticut Baptist Association. The Danbury Baptists had heard a rumor that the Congregationalist Denomination was destined to become the national denomination. Jefferson answered their fear in a letter assuring them there was no basis for their fear. He told them that the First Amendment built a wall of separation between church and state. Wallbuilders.com, 2008.

The snowball of subsequent cases, embellishments, and assumptions resulted in fear of the mere mention of God in public schools, leaving two subsequent generations ignorant of God's Word and even biblical history.

32 In Ephesians 6:12-17, the believer is instructed to put on the full armor of God in order to stand firm against the schemes of the evil one (Satan). The breastplate of righteousness and the sword of the spirit (The only offensive weapon, also known as the word of God) are two pieces of the armor.

33 Matthew 7:13-14.

34 Matthew 6:33

35 https://www.foxnews.com/video/6331340547112

36 James M. Black, *When the Roll is Called up Yonder*, 1893.

37 https://www.christianity.com/wiki/bible/who-is-baal-in-the-bible.html

38 https://www.learnreligions.com/asherah-in-the-bible-6824125

39 Spiritual Gifts Survey. Provided with permission by Lifeway Christian Resources, revised 2022. https://s7d9.scene7.com/is/content/LifeWayChristianResources/Spiritual_Gifts_Assessmentpdf.

Spiritual Gifts Survey

DIRECTIONS

This is not a test, so there are no wrong answers. The Spiritual Gifts Survey consists of 80 statements. Some items reflect concrete actions, other items are descriptive traits, and still others are statements of belief.

- Select one response you feel best characterizes yourself and place that number in the blank provided. Record your answer in the blank beside each item.
- Do not spend too much time on any one item. Remember, it is not a test. Usually your immediate response is best.
- Please give an answer for each item. Do not skip any items.
- Do not ask others how they are answering or how they think you should answer.
- Work at your own pace.

Your response choices are:

5 — Highly characteristic of me/definitely true of me
4 — Most of the time this would describe me/be true for me
3 — Frequently characteristic of me/true for me - about 50 percent of the time
2 — Occasionally characteristic of me/true of me 25 percent of the time
1 — Not at all characteristic of me/definitely untrue of me

Spritual Gifts Survey (Continued)

_____ 1. I have the ability to organize ideas, resources, time, and people effectively.
_____ 2. I am willing to study and prepare for the task of teaching.
_____ 3. I am able to relate the truths of God to specific situations.
_____ 4. I have a God given ability to help others grow in their faith.
_____ 5. I possess a special ability to communicate the truth of salvation.
_____ 6. I have the ability to make critical decisions when necessary.
_____ 7. I am sensitive to the hurts of people.
_____ 8. I experience joy in meeting needs through sharing possessions.
_____ 9. I enjoy studying.
_____ 10. I have delivered God's message of warning and judgment.
_____ 11. I am able to sense the true motivation of persons and movements.
_____ 12. I have a special ability to trust God in difficult situations.
_____ 13. I have a strong desire to contribute to the establishment of new churches.
_____ 14. I take action to meet physical and practical needs rather than merely talking about or planning how to help.
_____ 15. I enjoy entertaining guests in my home
_____ 16. I can adapt my guidance to fit the maturity of those working with me.
_____ 17. I can delegate and assign meaningful work.
_____ 18. I have an ability and desire to teach.
_____ 19. I am usually able to analyze a situation correctly.
_____ 20. I have a natural tendancy to encourage others.
_____ 21. I am willing to take the initiative in helping other Christians grow in their faith.
_____ 22. I have an acute awareness of other people's emotions, such as loneliness, pain, fear, and anger.
_____ 23. I am a cheerful giver.
_____ 24. I spend time digging into facts.
_____ 25. I feel like I have a message from God to deliver to others.
_____ 26. I can recognize when a person is genuine/honest.

Sprital Gifts Survey (Continued)

_____ 27. I am a person of vision (a clear mental portrait of a preferable future given by God). I am able to communicate vision in such a way that others commit to making the vision a reality.
_____ 28. I am willing to yield to God's will rather than question and waver.
_____ 29. I would like to be more active in getting the gospel to people in other countries.
_____ 30. It makes me happy to do things for people in need.
_____ 31. I am successful in getting a group to do its work joyfully.
_____ 32. I am able to make strangers feel at ease.
_____ 33. I have the ability to teach to a variety of different learning styles.
_____ 34. I can identify those who need encouragement.
_____ 35. I have trained Christians to be more obedient disciples of Christ.
_____ 36. I am willing to do whatever it takes to see others come to Christ.
_____ 37. I am drawn to people who are hurting.
_____ 38. I am a generous giver.
_____ 39. I am able to discover new truths in Scripture.
_____ 40. I have spiritual insights from Scripture concerning issues and people that compel me to speak out.
_____ 41. I can sense when a person is acting in accordance with God's will.
_____ 42. I can trust God even when things look dark.
_____ 43. I can determine where God wants a group to go and help it get there.
_____ 44. I have a strong desire to take the gospel to places where it has never been heard.
_____ 45. I enjoy reaching out to new people in my church and community.
_____ 46. I am sensitive to the needs of people.
_____ 47. I have been able to make effective and efficient plans for accomplishing the goals of a group.

SPRITUAL GIFTS SURVEY (CONTINUED)

_____ 48. I often am consulted when fellow Christians are struggling to make difficult decisions.
_____ 49. I think about how I can comfort and encourage others in my congregation.
_____ 50. I am able to give spiritual direction to others.
_____ 51. I am able to present the gospel to lost persons in such a way that they accept the Lord and His salvation.
_____ 52. I possess an unusual capacity to understand the feelings of those in distress.
_____ 53. I have a strong sense of stewardship based on the recognition that God owns all things.
_____ 54. I have deliverd to other persons messages that have come directly from God.
_____ 55. I can sense when a person is acting under God's leadership.
_____ 56. I try to be in God's will continually and be available for His use.
_____ 57. I feel that I should take the gospel to people who have different beliefs from me.
_____ 58. I have an acute awareness of the physical needs of others.
_____ 59. I am skilled in setting forth positive and precise steps of action.
_____ 60. I like to meet visitors at church and make them feel welcome.
_____ 61. I explain Scripture in such a way that others understand it.
_____ 62. I can usually see spiritual solutions to problems.
_____ 63. I welcome opportunities to help people who need comfort, consolation, encouragement, and counseling.
_____ 64. I feel at ease in sharing Christ with nonbelievers.
_____ 65. I can influence others to perform to their highest God-given potential.
_____ 66. I recognize the signs of stress and distress in others.
_____ 67. I desire to give generously and unpretentiously to worthwhile projects and ministries.
_____ 68. I can organize facts into meaningful relationships.
_____ 69. God gives me messages to deliver to His people.
_____ 70. I am able to sense whether people are being honest when they tell of their religious experiences.

Spritual Gifts Survey (Continued)

_____ 71. I enjoy presenting the gospel to persons of other cultures and backgrounds.
_____ 72. I enjoy doing little things that help people.
_____ 73. I can give a clear, uncomplicated presentation of the gospel.
_____ 74. I have been able to apply biblical truth to the specific needs of my church.
_____ 75. God has used me to encourage others to live Christlike lives.
_____ 76. I have sensed the need to help other people become more effective in their ministries.
_____ 77. I like to talk about Jesus to those who do not know Him.
_____ 78. I have the ability to make strangers feel comfortable in my home.
_____ 79. I have a wide range of study resources and know how to secure information.
_____ 80. I feel assured that a situation will change for the glory of God even when the situation seems impossible.

Scoring Your Survey

Follow these directions to figure your score for each spiritual gift.
1. Place in each box your numerical response (1-5) to the item number which is indicated below the box.
2. For each gift, add the numbers in the boxes and put the total in the TOTAL box.

Leadership	___ Item 6	+ ___ Item 16	+ ___ Item 27	+ ___ Item 43	+ ___ Item 65	+ ___ TOTAL
Administration	___ Item 1	+ ___ Item 17	+ ___ Item 31	+ ___ Item 47	+ ___ Item 59	+ ___ TOTAL
Teaching	___ Item 2	+ ___ Item 18	+ ___ Item 33	+ ___ Item 61	+ ___ Item 73	+ ___ TOTAL
Knowledge	___ Item 9	+ ___ Item 24	+ ___ Item 39	+ ___ Item 68	+ ___ Item 79	+ ___ TOTAL
Wisdom	___ Item 3	+ ___ Item 19	+ ___ Item 48	+ ___ Item 62	+ ___ Item 74	+ ___ TOTAL
Prophecy	___ Item 10	+ ___ Item 25	+ ___ Item 40	+ ___ Item 54	+ ___ Item 69	+ ___ TOTAL
Discernment	___ Item 11	+ ___ Item 26	+ ___ Item 41	+ ___ Item 55	+ ___ Item 70	+ ___ TOTAL
Exhortation	___ Item 20	+ ___ Item 34	+ ___ Item 49	+ ___ Item 63	+ ___ Item 75	+ ___ TOTAL
Shepherding	___ Item 4	+ ___ Item 21	+ ___ Item 35	+ ___ Item 50	+ ___ Item 76	+ ___ TOTAL
Faith	___ Item 12	+ ___ Item 28	+ ___ Item 42	+ ___ Item 56	+ ___ Item 80	+ ___ TOTAL
Evangelism	___ Item 5	+ ___ Item 36	+ ___ Item 51	+ ___ Item 64	+ ___ Item 77	+ ___ TOTAL
Apostleship	___ Item 13	+ ___ Item 29	+ ___ Item 44	+ ___ Item 57	+ ___ Item 71	+ ___ TOTAL
Service/Helps	___ Item 14	+ ___ Item 30	+ ___ Item 46	+ ___ Item 58	+ ___ Item 72	+ ___ TOTAL
Mercy	___ Item 7	+ ___ Item 22	+ ___ Item 37	+ ___ Item 52	+ ___ Item 66	+ ___ TOTAL
Giving	___ Item 8	+ ___ Item 23	+ ___ Item 38	+ ___ Item 53	+ ___ Item 67	+ ___ TOTAL
Hospitality	___ Item 15	+ ___ Item 32	+ ___ Item 45	+ ___ Item 60	+ ___ Item 78	+ ___ TOTAL

SANDRA F. MCCLURE

Graphing Your Profile

1. For each gift place a mark across the line at the point that corresponds to your TOTAL for that gift.
2. For each gift shade the line to the left of the mark that you have drawn.
3. The resultant graph gives a picture of your gifts. Gifts for which the bars are long are the ones in which you appear to be strongest. Gifts for which the bars are very short are the ones in which you appear not to be strong.

Now that you have completed the survey, thoughtfully answer the following questions.

The gifts I have begun to discover in my life are:
1. _____
2. _____
3. _____

- After prayer and worship, I am beginning to sense that God wants me to use my spiritual gifts to serve Christ's body by _____.
- I am not sure yet how God wants me to use my gifts to serve others. But I am committed to prayer and worship, seeking wisdom and opportunities to use the gifts I have received from God.

Ask God to help you know how He has gifted you for service and how you can begin to use this gift in ministry to others.

Notes/Citations (continued)

40 MacArthur, John. 2006. The MacArthur Study Bible. Thomas Nelson, Inc., 1600.

41 Harold McWhorter, *Sin will take you Farther*, 1945.

About the Author

Sandra F. McClure has had a passion for writing since sixth grade. As an adult, she discovered her passion for writing about the Lord. She has published three children's books: *Things I Ponder*, *Jack and the Creekside Miracle*, and a book co-authored with her two sisters called *The Chipmunk Family Odyssey*. Her children's books are designed to foster awe and intrigue for God's omnipotence and His natural world. They also edify the family, model respect for authority, and encourage empathy toward others – things that are sadly missing from childhood education today.

Sandra has been a corporate manager, an entrepreneur, and a Language Arts teacher. She has taught Sunday school and Bible skills to children for over thirty years. For the last decade, her spare time has been filled writing everything from poetry to sitcoms.

She and her husband, Bill, have been married for thirty-seven years. They have one daughter and three grandchildren.

Printed in the USA
CPSIA information can be obtained
at www.ICGtesting.com
LVHW010055230224
772600LV00007B/146